DISPELLING
MISCONCEPTIONS
About English Language Learners

Barbara
Gottschalk

DISPELLING
MISCONCEPTIONS
About English Language Learners

Research–Based Ways
to Improve Instruction

ASCD® | Alexandria, Virginia USA

1703 N. Beauregard St. • Alexandria, VA 22311-1714 USA
Phone: 800-933-2723 or 703-578-9600 • Fax: 703-575-5400
Website: www.ascd.org • E-mail: member@ascd.org
Author guidelines: www.ascd.org/write

Ronn Nozoe, *Interim CEO and Executive Director;* Stefani Roth, *Publisher;* Genny Ostertag, *Director, Content Acquisitions;* Susan Hills, *Acquisitions Editor;* Julie Houtz, *Director, Book Editing & Production;* Joy Scott Ressler, *Editor;* Judi Connelly, *Senior Art Director;* Mary Duran, *Graphic Designer;* Cynthia Stock, *Typesetter;* Kelly Marshall, *Interim Manager, Production Services;* Shajuan Martin, *E-Publishing Specialist;* Tristan Coffelt, *Production Specialist*

All web links in this book are correct as of the publication date below but may have become inactive or otherwise modified since that time. If you notice a deactivated or changed link, please e-mail books@ascd.org with the words "Link Update" in the subject line. In your message, please specify the web link, the book title, and the page number on which the link appears.

PAPERBACK ISBN: 978-1-4166-2828-6   ASCD product #120010   n10/19
PDF E-BOOK ISBN: 978-1-4166-2830-9; see Books in Print for other formats.

Quantity discounts are available: e-mail programteam@ascd.org or call 800-933-2723, ext. 5773, or 703-575-5773. For desk copies, go to www.ascd.org/deskcopy.

Library of Congress Cataloging-in-Publication Data

Names: Gottschalk, Barbara, author.
Title: Dispelling misconceptions about English language learners: research-based ways to improve instruction / by Barbara Gottschalk.
Description: Alexandria, VA, USA: ASCD, [2019] | Includes bibliographical references and index.
Identifiers: LCCN 2019015920 (print) | LCCN 2019981229 (ebook) | ISBN 9781416628286 (pbk.: alk. paper) | ISBN 9781416628309 (PDF)
Subjects: LCSH: English language—Study and teaching—Foreign speakers--Methods.
Classification: LCC PE1128.A2 G66 2019 (print) | LCC PE1128.A2 (ebook) | DDC 420.71—dc23
LC record available at https://lccn.loc.gov/2019015920
LC ebook record available at https://lccn.loc.gov/2019981229

28 27 26 25 24 23 22 21 20   1 2 3 4 5 6 7 8 9 10 11 12

This is dedicated to the teachers and English language learners whose comments, missteps, and triumphs appear in the following pages. You made me a better teacher and this a better book.

DISPELLING MISCONCEPTIONS
About English Language Learners

Acknowledgments

I'd like to thank my sister, Kathleen Andrews, who read and commented on the first drafts of this book. My husband, Cemil Ulus, never quite understood why I happily spent so many hours at the computer writing but always offered encouragement and support. My development editor, Susan Hills, provided valuable feedback in the later stages of writing. Terry Pruett-Said, my colleague from our days together at Kansas State University's English Language Program, was always available for ELL shop talk. I'm also grateful to my K–12 colleague, Helene Popovich, who kept telling me to "write it all down" whenever I shared yet another teaching story with her. A final thank-you goes to my former principal, Dr. Pat Cavanaugh, who started it all by suggesting, "You know, Barbara, you ought to write a book . . . ."

Introduction

My foreign-born husband and I had just returned to our apartment after attending his U.S. citizenship ceremony. It had been a big day for Cemil but a big one for me too. The whole event, including the swearing in, judge's remarks, and happy faces of new U.S. citizens from many different countries had genuinely touched me. When we met our downstairs neighbor in the hallway, I couldn't resist sharing the news: "Guess what, Mr. LeMaster? Cemil became a U.S. citizen today!" Our neighbor smiled broadly at my husband and replied, "Congratulations! Now you can pay taxes like the rest of us!" Of course, Cemil had always been paying taxes—the pay stub from his job certainly proved that. His citizenship status had nothing to do with whether he paid taxes or not. Our neighbor was happy for my husband and commented out of no ill will, but the facts about immigration and U.S. citizenship didn't back up his opinion. Much like our misinformed downstairs neighbor, many well-meaning teachers have misconceptions about English language learners (ELLs). This book will use research to debunk these *wrong* assumptions and show you how to make your teaching *right* for your ELLs.

If you are a K–12 teacher in the United States, you have probably taught an ELL. According to the Migration Policy Institute, the foreign-born share of the U.S. population is at its highest level since 1910, representing 13.5 percent of the overall population (Batalova & Alperin, 2018). The National Center for Education Statistics (NCES, 2011b) tells us over half (56 percent) of the nation's public school teachers have had at least one ELL in their classrooms. In addition, nearly three-fourths (74 percent) of our public schools enroll at least one ELL. If you plan to become a teacher, you should prepare to teach these students too. The Every Student Succeeds Act (Section 3121) signed into law in 2015 puts an even greater focus on ELLs, since both their achievement and their progress toward proficiency are included in accountability measures. That means all teachers need to know how to help their ELLs reach full academic English proficiency as quickly as possible.

If ELL numbers are increasing, then the number of teachers trained to work with them should be increasing as well. Data from the U.S. Department of Education tell us this is happening but not nearly fast enough to keep up with demand. In 2015–2016, 9.5 percent of K–12 students were English as a second language (ESL)/bilingual; in contrast, only 2.1 percent of K–12 teachers were ESL/bilingual teachers (NCES, 2017). The U.S. Department of Education (2018) reported that 33 states had teaching shortages in the area of ESL/ESL specialist. A national survey showed just 38 percent of public school teachers reported taking coursework to prepare them to teach ELLs before their first year of teaching (NCES, 2018a). Specialized training is critical for secondary teachers who often have long-term ELLs hiding in plain sight in their classrooms; it's even more critical for elementary teachers. If ELLs can reach proficiency before they leave elementary school, they'll be far more likely to graduate from high school and achieve on a par with non-ELLs on standardized assessments (Thompson, 2015).

ELLS master basic social English relatively quickly and can appear fluent to their teachers. In my experience, general education teachers tend to be more aware of and thus more concerned about meeting the needs of ELLs who are recent immigrants at basic English proficiency levels. However, teachers must also be mindful of the intermediate and advanced ELLs in their classrooms whose needs may go unnoticed. These students don't need short-term targeted interventions or pullout instruction with an ESL specialist; a trained, knowledgeable general education teacher can support them just as effectively and more efficiently in the mainstream classroom. Long-term ELLs, those students who have been learning English for five or more years without being reclassified as former ELLs, make up more than half of secondary ELLs (National Clearinghouse for English Language Acquisition, 2015). Elementary teachers can help their secondary colleagues meet this challenge by ensuring ELLs get off to a good start in the elementary years. Helping ELLs reach full proficiency, then, is a top priority for teachers at both the elementary and secondary levels.

This book originated as a response to my colleagues' requests for help with their ELLs. These general education teachers often had *experience* teaching ELLs but, unfortunately, not much *knowledge* of how to do it well. They were perceptive enough to be aware of the needs of their newcomers but often didn't realize, for example, that a 3rd grade student born in the United States could also be an ELL. This lack of specific knowledge is not unusual. Research by the Education Commission of the States (2014a) shows my state, Michigan, is one of 36 states not requiring any specialized training for teachers with ELLs in their classrooms beyond this vague guidance in a U.S. Department of Education (2015) Dear Colleague letter: "At a minimum, every school district is responsible for ensuring that there is an adequate number of teachers to instruct EL students and that these teachers have mastered the skills necessary to effectively teach in the district's program for EL students" (p. 14). This book will help you, a teacher of ELLs, master those skills.

"I do that!" whispered a colleague to me during a professional development session about teaching ELLs. Attendance at this summer workshop was voluntary, but my colleague was there because the numbers of ELLs in her classes had increased, and she wanted more information about how to teach them. Her revelation was that much of what she was doing already made sense for ELLs too. The workshop was simply making her more mindful of doing so in the future. This book will do the same thing. In many cases, I'll point out the reasons why what you're doing already can work with ELLs as well. In other cases, I'll use research to show you why it's better for ELLs to do it a different way. Countless books and articles have been written about all the topics covered in this book. I've read many of them—so you don't have to—and distilled the relevant information you need to help your ELLs.

The examples and vignettes highlighted in this book came from the classrooms of all kinds of teachers—young and old, effective and less effective, experienced and inexperienced. Some positive examples and negative examples even came from the same classroom, mine included. Teachers always have, still do, and will continue to make mistakes. Smart teachers, however, learn from their mistakes, and really smart teachers learn from other teachers' mistakes! Perceptive teachers realize when things aren't working out in their classrooms. Knowledgeable teachers not only realize this but also are more likely to know *why* things didn't go as well as planned. Reading this book will help you become more knowledgeable. The ELLs in your classroom will benefit too.

Just Who Is an English Language Learner?

MISCONCEPTION: "HE'S NOT AN ELL. HE WAS BORN HERE."

Can you pick out the two ELLs, the former ELL, and the three never ELLs in Figure 1.1? You can't—and that's the point.

FIGURE 1.1 WHO IS THE ELL?

This chapter will give you information about how ELLs are identified and assessed. You'll also learn about ELL population trends and recent demographic changes. Education, like real estate, is local. If you're a high school science teacher in Nebraska with five intermediate ELLs in your Biology 1 class, the situation in California may not seem particularly relevant to you. Still, learning about trends in other states or even in other parts of your own state will help you make sense of what's happening—or going to happen—where you teach. You and your classroom can then be prepared!

The Problem with This Misconception

Let's unpack this misconception by taking an inventory of our own assumptions and (mis)understandings about ELLs. This will help you activate any prior knowledge you may have. Using simple anticipation guides like this one is an easy way to prepare your own students before a lesson or a unit of study. The following quiz might help you discover some misconceptions of your own after learning the correct answers:

- A limited English proficient (LEP) student is the same as an English language learner (ELL). True or False?

- The majority of K–12 ELLs were born in the United States. True or False?

- Approximately what percentage of all K–12 students in the United States are ELLs?
    - ❏ 10
    - ❏ 15
    - ❏ 5
    - ❏ 20

- For approximately what percentage of ELLs nationwide is Spanish the home language?
  - ❑ 50
  - ❑ 95
  - ❑ 75
  - ❑ 85

- Which state has the largest percentage of students enrolled as ELLs?
  - ❑ North Carolina
  - ❑ Texas
  - ❑ Florida
  - ❑ California

- The percentage of ELLs is highest in the middle grades. True or False?

- By how much did the population of ELLs as a proportion of the total K–12 school population in the United States *increase* from 2000 to 2015?
  - ❑ 15.9 percent
  - ❑ 10.1 percent
  - ❑ 5.5 percent
  - ❑ 1.4 percent

- Which state has experienced the largest percentage increase in ELLs in the past 10 years?
  - ❑ Kansas
  - ❑ California
  - ❑ Arizona
  - ❑ Texas

- Students born in the United States are exempt from taking an English language proficiency test. True or False?

- Every state has a different English language proficiency test. True or False?

The Reasons Behind the Correct Answers

Learning about the reasons behind the correct answers to anticipation guide questions is a good way to wrap up learning at the
end of any unit or lesson. We'll do the same thing with the questions you've just answered.

A Limited English Proficient (LEP) Student Is the Same as an English Language Learner (ELL).

True. The federal government still uses LEP, but the acronym
isn't as common as it used to be—mainly because it describes students in negative terms. Another descriptor you may encounter
is FLEP (former limited English proficient). This term describes
students who are proficient and no longer LEP. LEP and FLEP
are *adjectives* describing a particular kind of student; ELL and EL
(English learner) refer to *the student*. (I prefer using ELL and will
do so throughout this book.) Other acronyms describing *what
is taught* to ELLs are ESL (English as a second language); ESOL
(English for speakers of other languages); and even ENL (English
as a new language), which is used in the state of New York. ESOL
commonly appears in K–12 settings and is a more accurate term
for multilingual students. For example, in my corner of Michigan, many children speak both Arabic and Chaldean in the home.
That being the case, English is not simply the second language
of these children—it's the third language they're learning. You'll
notice "ESL" is used more often in adult education settings and
the like (which may be a way to distinguish it from English as a
foreign language [EFL: what adult students may have learned in
their home countries]). When teaching in Japan, I taught EFL to
my students because it was outside an English-speaking country.
When teaching Japanese students in the United States, I taught
English as a *second* language (ESL). The only thing that changed
was the setting in which I taught English.

The Majority of K–12 ELLs Were Born in the United States.

True. This is a common misconception about ELLs. The percentage of *foreign-born* ELLs is higher at the secondary level (38 percent) than it is at the elementary level (15 percent). These small percentages of foreign-born ELLs show that the overwhelming majority of all ELLs were born in the United States (Zong & Batalova, 2015).

Approximately What Percentage of All K–12 Students in the United States Are ELLs?

10. According to the National Center for Education Statistics (2018d), 9.5 percent of U.S. public school students were ELLs in fall 2015, and the percentage was trending upward. Education is so local, however, that we tend to forget the big national picture. Also, the overall average masks the big differences in various parts of the United States. ELLs aren't spread evenly throughout the United States; statistics show that 60 percent of the ELLs in K–12 schools are in the five states with the highest ELL populations: California, Texas, Florida, New York, and Illinois (Office of English Language Acquisition, 2018).

For Approximately What Percentage of ELLs Nationwide is Spanish the Home Language?

75. According to the National Center for Education Statistics (2018d), 3.7 million ELLs, or 77 percent of the total ELL population, speak Spanish. The next most common languages are Arabic, Chinese, and Vietnamese—spoken by 109,000, 104,000, and 85,300 students, respectively. The ELL population is linguistically diverse; at least 350 languages are spoken in U.S. homes (U.S. Census Bureau, 2015). My own teaching situation is a good example of this diversity. While a majority of ELLs at my school come from homes where Arabic is spoken, the other ELLs speak 27 different home languages. Many other settings are similar. When people learn that I teach ELLs, they often make two assumptions: (1) I'm bilingual and (2) I speak Spanish. Neither is correct. It's often true that ELL teachers speak one of the native languages of their students—and in many cases this is Spanish—but don't assume it's always so. Also, commonly spoken languages in your school district can change. My school district in Michigan has had a majority of Arabic-speaking ELLs for quite some time, but the second most common home language changed from Albanian to Bengali during the years I taught there. The bilingual Polish-speaking ELL teacher who had been hired 25 years earlier, when the community had more Polish-speaking residents, had very few Polish-speaking ELLs in her classes by the end of her career in the district. She then relied less on her bilingual Polish skills to provide native language support and more on her training in how to teach ELLs.

Which State Has the Largest Percentage of Students Enrolled as ELLs?

California. California is home to one-third of our nation's ELLs, according to the most recent statistics, and it has both the largest absolute number of ELLs (more than 1.3 million) and the highest percentage of ELLs (21 percent) compared to total enrollment (NCES, 2018c).

The Percentage of ELLs Is Highest in the Middle Grades.

False. The percentage of ELLs in each grade decreases steadily throughout the grades. The highest percentage is in kindergarten, nearly four times greater than the percentage in grade 12 (NCES, 2018d). This finding could have two causes. First, since most ELLs are born in the United States, they naturally show up in the greatest numbers in kindergarten, when they begin school. If everything goes well, they will reach proficiency by the time they enter middle school and will no longer be counted as ELLs. Second, immigrant children tend to be young. Over half of foreign-born children in the United States are elementary school age (The Urban Institute, 2019).

By How Much Did the Population of ELLs as a Proportion of the Total K–12 School Population in the United States *Increase* from 2000 to 2015?

1.4 percentage points. Although the percentage of ELLs as a proportion of the total school population nationally didn't increase dramatically over 15 years, 19 states doubled their percentages of ELLs as a proportion of their total school populations (NCES, 2018c). The foreign-born population of the United States is increasing, so this is one cause (Batalova & Alperin, 2018). Also, the percentage of ELLs may be increasing as a result of better identification or because students are remaining ELLs longer. If the number of ELLs in your district is increasing, it's important to figure out why. Are more newcomers enrolling, or are your ELLs remaining ELLs and not being reclassified? You'll learn how to respond to each of these situations later in this book.

Which State Has Experienced the Greatest Percentage Increase in ELLs in the Past 10 Years?

Kansas. According to the National Center for Education Statistics (2018c), Kansas was the state with the greatest *increase* in ELLs over the past 10 years. ELLs as a percentage of the total school population more than doubled, from 5.2 percent in 2005 to 10.6 percent in 2015. A relatively sudden increase of ELLs in schools with little previous experience in educating them puts the need for professional development into sharp focus. This is not necessarily a bad thing. Teachers in school districts with a long history of having ELLs may be confident they're meeting the needs of their ELLs simply because they have experience in teaching them. This may be a false sense of confidence, however, if it's not supported by adequate progress of their ELLs. In contrast, teachers in schools with a sudden increase in ELLs may be more likely to realize what they don't know and thus see the need for professional development. For example, the tiny school district in rural northwestern Kansas I attended as a child historically had 0 percent ELLs. It then experienced an increase in its ELL population to 30 percent by 2017. I had a chance to discuss these changes with a former classmate, a teacher in this district, at a high school reunion. As I listened to her talk about the professional development she and her colleagues were getting in response to this change, I couldn't help noticing how she saw this change as a positive opportunity, not a negative challenge. She correctly realized that new ELLs moving into the district could keep the school in her rural community from closing due to low enrollment. It's important to keep track of similar trends in ELL numbers in your district, so that resources can be allocated where they're most needed.

Students Born in the United States Are Exempt from Taking an English Language Proficiency Test.

False. According to the U.S. Department of Education (2016), "[a limited English proficient] student, or English language learner (ELL), is defined as an individual

- who was not born in the United States, or
- whose native language is a language other than English, or
- who comes from an environment where a language other than English is dominant, or
- who is an American Indian or Alaska Native and who comes from an environment where a language other than English has had a significant impact on his or her level of English language proficiency" (p. 43).

As you can see from this definition, being born outside the United States is just one of several ways a student may qualify as an ELL. Students are screened for English language proficiency depending on how their parents answer the questions on a home language survey when they register their children for school. The U.S. Department of Education (2017) suggests the following three questions as "minimally compliant under the law" (p. 4):

- What is the primary language used in the home, regardless of the language spoken by the student?
- What is the language most often spoken by the student?
- What is the language that the student first acquired?

If a parent answers one or more of these questions with a language other than English, the child is then screened for English proficiency. This is often not stated on the form, so parents may not realize the consequences of their answers. If parents do understand what comes next, they may answer home language survey questions with "English" to avoid additional testing or to keep their children out of ESL or bilingual classes they feel will hold back their progress. This first concern is a valid one. If a child's performance on the English language proficiency screener determines he is an ELL, the child will be tested annually until reaching proficiency. Parents can't opt their children out of this testing. Parents can, however, opt their children out of ESL or bilingual services if they fear such services or classes will hamper their children's progress.

In spite of this guidance from the U.S. Department of Education, home language survey questions can vary greatly from state to state and district to district (Education Commission of the States, 2014b). For example, following are the home language survey questions from a school district in Michigan:

- Is your child's native tongue a language other than English? If yes, what language?
- Is the primary language used in your child's home or environment a language other than English?

Another example comes from a school district in Florida:

- Is a language other than English used in the home?
- Does the student have a first language other than English?
- Does the student most frequently speak a language other than English?

A third example comes from a school district in Texas:

• What language is spoken in your home most of the time?
• What language does your child speak most of the time?

As you can see, even with translation, these very different questions are open to various interpretations. What, exactly, is a "native" language? How often is "frequently"? And under what circumstances does a language become the "primary" one in a home? It wouldn't be unreasonable for a parent to give different answers to home language survey questions for the same child if the child were registering in different school districts. In addition to this parent interpretation, a final example of a home language survey from a school district in North Carolina adds teacher subjectivity. Here, the ESL teacher is asked to "review the responses, interview the parent as necessary, and/or observe the student to determine the home language." These examples from four different states illustrate how inconsistent the process can be for determining who will be screened for English language proficiency. Add to this the fact that exit requirements for reclassifying ELLs vary among states, and you can see we are far from a national definition of an ELL. This doesn't help when trying to compare states or make sense of national trends, but what's important for you as an individual teacher is to learn what the identification process is like in your own district. Understanding this is a factor you can control.

Each State Has Its Own English Language Proficiency Test.

False. States differ, but not completely so. The nearest thing we have to a national English proficiency test is the WIDA ACCESS for ELLs 2.0, which is given in 39 states and U.S. territories. Another assessment, the ELPA21, is given in an additional seven states. Another seven states, mostly those with high numbers of ELLs, such as California and Texas, have their own English language proficiency tests. The good thing about many states using the same English proficiency assessment is that it generates large amounts of data on a wide range of ELLs; that's useful for comparisons, something that's not possible with individual state assessments. The Appendix provides a list of the English language proficiency tests used in each state and the District of Columbia. All these tests must annually measure an ELL's proficiency in the four language domains: listening, speaking, reading, and writing.

Setting This Misconception Straight

You've already made a start by taking the quiz and discovering any misconceptions you may have had. A key point to remember is that "English Language Learner" can refer to a wide variety of students. Most of us realize ELLs speak different languages, but they can also come from very different socioeconomic backgrounds and have different levels of academic preparation. Let's meet some ELLs who represent this diversity.

NOORA

Noora is an 18-year-old high school senior who was born in Iraq. She arrived in the United States two and a half years ago with her family after spending several years living in exile in Jordan. She attends a large suburban high school with a sizeable ELL population. Noora worries about catching up, since she wasn't able to attend school consistently in Jordan. Noora is a good student and, in less than three years, is coming close to reaching English proficiency. She wants to become an engineer, so she has her sights set on taking AP classes in her senior year to prepare for college. Unfortunately, her school requires students to exit ELL status before taking AP classes. She's hoping to be the exception to this rule.

CAN

Can is a 1st grade student from Turkey living temporarily in the United States while his parents study for graduate degrees at a large state university in a rural college town. Little Can likes school, but his classmates tease him about his name. In Turkish, Can's name is pronounced like "John," but his classmates mispronounce it on purpose, calling him "Tin Can." Can's teacher wonders if she should suggest Can begin spelling his name "the American way" as John. The teacher doesn't realize she's missing a golden opportunity to teach all of her students some valuable lessons in linguistic diversity. Can's parents (or a quick Internet search) could tell her that "c" is pronounced like "j" in Turkish. She could point this out to the class and ask students to find other examples of names with interesting pronunciations. While the reason for his teasing is unique because of his Turkish name, the experience Can is having is similar to that of many other students who are made to feel different for various reasons. Like students everywhere, Can just wants to fit in.

LULJETA

Luljeta is a recent high school graduate and has enrolled in the local community college. She came to the United States from Albania as a 5th grader and reached a high intermediate level of English proficiency by the end of 8th grade. She continued to take her state's annual test of English proficiency every year throughout high school, but neither she nor her parents paid much attention to the results since she was getting good grades in her regular academic classes. She's irritated she was placed into a developmental ESL course at the local community college. "I don't need ESL," she tells her instructor. "I speak English all the time." When her instructor tries to explain her placement test results, she gets confused. "You mean this test counted?" she asks. Luljeta suffers from an honesty gap, the distance between her academic hopes and her actual preparation. Hopefully, that gap won't prove too great to achieve her goal of becoming a nurse.

REGINA

Regina is a newly arrived 5th grade student from Mexico with basic English proficiency. She is reading on grade level in Spanish and has a good academic record from her school in Mexico. Her father is on a two-year temporary work assignment in the United States for a large international company. When he was Regina's age, he had a chance to attend U.S. schools for several years when his own father had a temporary work assignment in the United States. Regina's father gained a lot from that experience, and he wants the same for Regina. Her teachers might be tempted to underestimate Regina and water down her lessons—after all, they think, her English is basic—but that would be a mistake. She's capable of accessing the curriculum with support.

EDUARDO

Eduardo is a 19-year-old high school senior from Honduras. He and his older brother have been living in a small town in the southern United States for three years. He studies hard at school and also works hard at a nearly full-time job at a local chicken processing plant. He works so hard, in fact, he sometimes has trouble completing his homework and staying awake in school. He is at a high

intermediate level of proficiency and is on track to graduate from high school. His career goal is to become a super-
visor at the plant where he now works part time.

YOUSIF

Little Yousif, a Chaldean-speaking student entering kindergarten, was born in the United States. His parents were
born in Iraq, so Yousif's family speaks Arabic as well as
their heritage language, Chaldean, in the home. Kindergarten is Yousif's first school experience; his grandmother
has been watching him ever since he was born while his
parents worked outside the home. Yousif's teacher also
taught his older brother and sister and is a bit disappointed. "Why didn't they teach him any English?" she
wonders to a colleague. Yousif's English vocabulary may
be zero, but his vocabulary is actually quite large when
what he knows in Arabic and Chaldean is counted. Yousif
has already been learning two languages in addition to
the English he will learn at school. Let's hope his teacher
eventually sees this as a plus.

NUR

Nur is an 11th grade Rohingya refugee from Myanmar. He
knows some Arabic from his religious training; he can also
understand Rohingya and Hindi, but he didn't learn to
read and write in either language. That's because he didn't
attend school in Myanmar or in the refugee settlement
in Indonesia, where he stayed for nearly three years. A
newcomer center is the most suitable option for Nur but,
lacking that, the principal at his new high school lobbied
to get Nur enrolled in the district's alternative high school
instead. "At least he won't hurt our graduation rate," the
principal tells himself.

These snapshots of various ELLs illustrate how diverse their backgrounds and academic preparation can be. Their stories also show the vastly different challenges ELLs face—and the challenges teachers and administrators face in meeting ELLs' needs and helping them reach their goals. One thing many ELLs have in common is that they are economically disadvantaged but, like the students described previously, for different reasons. The child of international graduate students studying in the United States may be temporarily economically disadvantaged, but it's not the kind of generational poverty other economically disadvantaged students endure. Similarly, an economically disadvantaged ELL may have immigrant parents who were educated professionals with good jobs in their home country. Their poverty here in the United States is situational. Many difficulties facing ELLs are actually due to factors such as poverty and transience, challenges they share with other at-risk students.

Making It Right in Your Classroom

- *Find out which English proficiency test your state uses.* Look at your ELLs' test results—are students weak in certain areas? Find out how long your students have been ELLs. Are they recent arrivals to the United States, or has all their education been in American schools?
- *Learn the acronyms describing your students.* Are your students ELLs, ELs, or LEP students? Will they be studying ESL, ESOL, or ENL until they are FLEP? Don't be afraid to ask what a particular term means.
- *Learn who your ELLs are, but don't call them out.* ELLs want to fit in. You'll get tips later about adapting your instruction to meet the needs of your ELLs without looking markedly different from what you're already doing for your other students. Your ELLs will appreciate this.
- *Make sure your perceptions match reality.* For example, a kindergarten teacher at my school once noted how it had become

much harder than it was five years earlier for her students to do independent center work while she met with reading groups. Her students seemed so needy now. As I listened to her, I thought, "Ah, increasing class size and a larger percentage of ELLs!" I started to suggest this to the teacher but wisely checked my records first. It's a good thing I did, because past class rosters showed, in fact, that this teacher's classes had always contained approximately 25 students. The number of ELLs had remained stable too. My explanation for her increased difficulties wasn't correct. What *had* increased in this kindergarten teacher's class was the percentage of students with special needs. Perceptions aren't always correct; that's why you need facts to back them up.

A LITTLE EXTRA . . .

For you data nerds, https://ncela.ed.gov/sources-english-learner-el-data has links to more than 10 additional websites offering reliable data on ELLs and immigration. Most of the links are to government websites such as the U.S. Census Bureau, but other organizations, such as the Migration Policy Institute, are also represented.

Conclusion

"I didn't speak any English when I started kindergarten, and we didn't have any ESL teachers like you back then to help," one of my teaching colleagues once said to me. She had successfully learned English without any special teachers, screening, or accommodations, so she felt ELLs nowadays should be able to do the same thing. She was right—some ELLs like her *did* master English on their own many years ago, but things have changed. Now, students are expected to meet increasingly high standards and schools are being held accountable for the progress of *all* of their students. That's why learning who your ELLs are is important. In addition, we are preparing our students for an increasingly global workplace, where they will need to collaborate across cultures, solve problems, and learn new skills. In this multicultural environment, your ELLs' bilingual skills will be an asset. In the next chapter, you'll learn additional reasons why maintaining the home language is important and how to help your ELLs do this.

Supporting Home Language Maintenance

MISCONCEPTION: "THE PROBLEM, MRS. CHEN, IS THAT YOU'RE SPEAKING CHINESE AT HOME."

The teacher who gave this advice to an ELL parent is not alone. Misconceptions abound related to the use of a child's home language. In this chapter, you'll learn how maintaining the home language actually helps students learn a second language such as English faster. You'll also get advice on how to support your students' home languages, even if you don't speak them yourself.

The Problem with This Misconception

"Ms. Gottschalk, I can speak Chaldean!" a 1st grade ELL once announced to me.

"You can?" I replied. "Good for you!"

"Yes," he continued. "That's why I can't read."

Ouch. I was horrified by this young student's perception of his bilingualism, but not surprised. He was simply reflecting misguided beliefs about second-language acquisition the adults around him held. The idea that speaking the home language at home is somehow a bad thing is the one misconception about second-language acquisition that has the most staying power. Like a cat with nine lives, it simply refuses to die, in spite of research to the contrary. Reflecting the thinking of the day nearly 100 years ago, Florence Goodenough (1926), developer of the Stanford Achievement Test, speculated whether "the use of a foreign language in the home is one of the chief factors in producing mental retardation" (p. 393). She concluded instead that the use of a foreign language in the home was probably a result, not a cause, of inferior intellectual ability.

Ouch again. Thankfully, research has changed our thinking since then. Now we know bilingualism, in and of itself, need not negatively affect English language development. In fact, many studies show bilingualism has a *positive* effect. In an analysis of 11 studies on family influences on English language learning, Genesee and Riches (2006) found that "[p]roficiency in the home language does not have to result in reduced English language skills and, conversely, the development of English language skills does not have to entail loss of the home language" (p. 142). What is crucial, they point out, is the development of *both* languages. It seems so intuitively logical—if everybody in the home, including parents, just spoke more English with each other, everyone would learn English faster! Practice makes perfect, right? If only it were that simple. Speaking English at home doesn't explain why some non-ELLs also have academic difficulties. In fact, conditions that put non-ELLs at risk, such as poverty, transience, and low parent engagement, can also apply to ELLs. Those factors are affecting their progress, not their bilingualism.

It *is* easier to keep the home language nowadays because it's much easier than it used to be to stay abreast of current events in the home country and access media in the home language. That's a good thing. Cable TV is available in multiple languages, and TV shows from the home country help home language maintenance. The Internet offers the same advantages in addition to providing reading material in many different languages. It's also far easier to communicate online in real time with extended family members in the home country. In spite of these technological advantages, it's still relatively easy for children to at least partially lose the home language.

I remember the poignant observations of a Romanian-speaking parent at my school. She was justifiably proud of how all the children in her family had become proficient in English, but it was sad to hear her describe how her youngest child couldn't communicate with extended family members back in Romania. It was obvious she felt sad too, and she admitted this had happened because it had become increasingly difficult to maintain the home language with the youngest child in the family. He had entered kindergarten with a higher level of English than his older brothers and sisters but, with the loss of bilingualism, at a significant social cost. Tellingly, his older brothers, even though they'd started at lower levels of English proficiency in kindergarten, had eventually reached full proficiency by 5th grade. They had done so while retaining their home language—the best of both linguistic worlds.

Another case illustrates how losing the home language may have contributed to a 3rd grade ELL's anger management problems. This student had reached an advanced level of English proficiency and was doing well academically, but digging deeper, we learned he didn't know his home language, Vietnamese, very well. An only child, he couldn't communicate in English with his parents or their adult friends because their English skills were limited. At the same time, they couldn't communicate with him very well in Vietnamese because his Vietnamese skills were limited. Can you imagine how frustrating this must have been for both him and his parents? No wonder he had trouble verbalizing his anger in an appropriate way.

Setting This Misconception Straight

My young student from the beginning of this chapter who attributed his reading difficulties to his bilingualism was only half right. He *was* still learning to read, but his bilingualism was an advantage, not an obstacle. If anything, this child's knowledge of Chaldean, his home language, was *helping* him learn to read in English, not hindering him. In its extensive review of the research done for the U.S. Department of Education on developing literacy in second language learners, the National Literacy Panel found clear evidence that drawing on first-language literacy skills can benefit English language learners (August, 2006). This applied to oral proficiency, as well as literacy, in the home language. Students who have a strong grounding in their native language are able to use those strengths to better master a new language such as English. For example, students who can read in their native language can transfer those skills to a new language, thus making it easier for them to learn to read in English (Genesee & Riches, 2006). Maintaining one's home language while learning English, then, is not a zero-sum game; learning both is a win-win situation. At the same time, lack of a strong home language base on which to build can produce unsatisfactory results in both languages. As a bilingual student in my friend's developmental ESL class at our local community college once mournfully put it, "I don't think I know any language very well."

You are not in your students' homes every day, but you can stress the importance of home language maintenance from your classroom. In particular, it's critical to educate parents who are being told to stop speaking their native language with their children and use English instead. As we've seen, this "language shaming" can harm students academically and impair family relationships. As the wise speech therapist at my school once explained to another teacher, "Good Arabic is better than bad English." Actually, good [insert any home language here] is better than bad English.

Children learn language through interaction with the adults in the home. Parents who are using the language they're most comfortable with will be more likely to have longer, richer discussions with their children. Stressing the importance of maintaining the home language will help your ELLs and also empower all the non-English-speaking adults in their homes. Many ELL parents have told me grandparents were the ones who helped keep the home language alive. Answering in English is not an option for children who need to communicate with a non-English-speaking grandma! A 1st grade ELL once told me: "My dad can speak English, but my mom, she don't know anything." I hope he meant his mom just didn't know any English, but I fear he was assuming not knowing English meant not knowing *anything*. We know that's wrong, but we need to show our students we understand that too. We can honor parents' knowledge by encouraging them to share that knowledge in their home language and making them feel comfortable doing so.

Making It Right in Your Classroom

The title of this heading may seem like a misnomer, since maintaining the home language is something done in the home, not the classroom. Still, you can help parents with this—maybe not in the classroom, but *from* the classroom. My own school, with students representing 27 different home languages, is a good example of a "super-diverse" school where many different languages are spoken. Your school may be super diverse, or your ELLs may have just one home language. As a teacher, though, your charge is to encourage all your ELLs to maintain their home languages, even if you don't speak those languages yourself. Here are some things you can do:

- *Encourage parents to talk with their children about what they're learning in school and to use academic vocabulary from their native language*. This is a good recommendation because it's easy for ELL parents to implement. Expecting ELL parents to speak English at home or help with social studies homework might encourage them to think, "I don't know English, so I guess I can't help my child." Putting parents in this position makes them "helpless and hopeless" because the focus is on what they can't do. Instead, create agency by focusing on what they *can* do. When teachers attribute an ELL's academic difficulties to "you know, they only speak [insert any home language here] at home," they're blaming, not explaining. It's not the language being spoken; it's that children aren't getting enough interaction with anybody in any language. Research has pointed out this is also the case with children who live in poverty (Suskind, 2015). We shouldn't shame parents for speaking their native language with their children. It's hard enough being a parent. Can you imagine how much more difficult it would be trying to do it in a language you're not comfortable using?

- *Honor the home language by using it, if necessary, when you interact with ELL parents.* Don't use children to interpret for you. It's just not best practice to ask anybody under the age of 18 to take on the role of an interpreter. Children won't have the appropriate vocabulary to participate in adult conversations in their native languages, let alone their second language. That's why it's disconcerting to learn that, in a random survey of 563 K–12 teachers, nearly half of them admitted to talking to an ELL parent through the student or an older sibling (ClassDojo, 2018). Use adult interpreters; if possible, use ones with specific training and experience. Like many other teachers, I've thought simply that speaking "easy English" would be enough, but I've learned differently. When I spoke easy English, parents would simply nod and say, "Yes, yes," but when I used an interpreter, parents asked more questions and made more comments. It's a good idea to have a third party interpret even if one parent speaks English because, otherwise, the other parent can be left out.

For example, after a parent–teacher conference, we assume the English-speaking parent tells the non-English-speaking parent what was said, but we can't be sure. A third-party interpreter can give both parents equal access to information. It lengthens a conference, but it empowers parents and teachers alike.

I used to think it wasn't a good idea to use online translation or an app like Google Translate, mainly because of the mangled translations I'd get, especially for languages with different writing systems, such as Japanese and Arabic. These apps are getting better, though, so now I'd say it's better than nothing. However, use of these apps should be limited to simple communications, such as asking about a field trip permission form or reminding parents of an after-school activity.

My own school district subscribes to a telephone language interpretation service, but even with training, teachers needed encouragement to use it. I saw the benefits of using that service, however, when I attended a parent–teacher conference with a teacher who had previously been reluctant to use it. At the end of the conference, when the teacher asked the interpreter on the phone if there was anything else the parent wanted to add, the parent asked the interpreter to thank the teacher. It was a simple request but imagine how good it must have made the parent feel to have his appreciation *fully and appropriately conveyed* to the teacher. We tend to forget that when we speak in English—even easy English—we're still operating from a position of power as the native speaker of English. Using interpretation equalizes the parent–teacher relationship by privileging communication on the parents' behalf as well.

- *Encourage language awareness.* Get information about your students' home languages. Ensure your classroom library has bilingual books in these languages. Bilingual books enjoyed high circulation from my classroom library. Make sure your school's media center also has bilingual books available in the home languages of your students. Books in the native language are also good for parents to have in their homes to read together with their children. The best books are those that children will be reading later in English in school or books that build background knowledge in the content areas. Do your best to make these kinds of books available to your students' parents or give them information on where they might find them. If you can't find books in your students' home languages, wordless picture books are a good alternative for discussion—in any language.

- *Establish and strengthen connections with community organizations to further home language development.* I once got a supply of hard-to-find Chaldean-English picture dictionaries from the priest at a local Chaldean Catholic church. You can imagine how happy Chaldean-speaking students were to find those books in my classroom library. Public libraries often stock bilingual materials in the languages of the local community. Ethnic and religious organizations also offer "Saturday school" or other classes to help children learn the language of the home country. Make sure your students and their families are aware of these resources.

- *Use the home language to ensure comprehension.* Are you pairing up new ELLs with a language buddy who can give them native language support? Be careful, though. Some ELLs have told me they were assigned language buddies but then were chastised for "talking" when they asked their seat partners about the lesson. Don't send that kind of double message.

- *Recognize and acknowledge your students' home languages.* My older Arabic-speaking students never failed to notice that I had on my desk a coffee mug with Arabic sayings on it that I had bought at a local international festival. Asking them, "Can you read any of these phrases?" was a low-stakes way to find out how literate they were in Arabic. Simple signals like multilingual welcome signs are a common way to elevate home languages, but extend this to deeper connections. For several years, my super-diverse school hosted an assembly that honored a language spoken by our students. One year it was a puppet play featuring the Russian version of *The Gingerbread Man*, and another year it was an opera about a Mexican folktale, *How Nanita Learned to Make Flan*. In still another year, professional actors helped a class of 2nd and 3rd graders dramatize an Arab folktale and then, together, presented it to the entire school. "Ms. G., they were speaking my language!" exclaimed one audience member after the performance. The culture, as well as the language, speaks to students.

* *Bring the home language into your classroom.* For example, invite parents into your classroom to do a bilingual read-aloud with the parent reading the foreign language part and you reading the English part of the story, preferably one from the target culture. An Arabic-English version of a Dr. Seuss story is one way to reach your Arabic-speaking students, for example, but using a bilingual version of a traditional Arabic folktale your students may already know is even better. Ask a parent to read aloud a short picture book entirely in the home language. Then show the pictures again and see if students can retell the story in English. Even students who don't understand the language of the picture book will be surprised at how much of the story they can understand through the pictures. This activity not only highlights a home language, but it also gives monolingual students an idea of what it's like for newcomers in an English class.

* *Ensure that secondary ELLs and former ELLs get credit for their home language.* Check to see if your state is one of the 35-plus states that have already adopted the Seal of Biliteracy, a designation that students can have added to their high school diplomas upon graduation. Although specific requirements vary by state and school district, in general the Seal of Biliteracy certifies that a student has attained a high intermediate level of proficiency in English and another language. Just as important, it validates an ELL's home language. Also, ensure high school ELLs get world language credit for their experience going to school in their native language before coming to the United States. Students may need to gather transcript information from as early as their upper elementary years, but it's worth it.

- *Start a heritage language book club.* This is an interesting option, especially at the secondary level. Often bilingual students aren't completely biliterate, especially if they've grown up in the United States. This means they can speak their home language but don't have literacy in their home language. Gathering students together to read a book in their native language can give them confidence as native speakers and also enhance their academic skills in their native language. This honors the home language and builds English language skills too!

A LITTLE EXTRA . . .

- Language Lizard (www.languagelizard.com) sells bilingual books with each page in both English and another language. The books are offered in a variety of languages and are mostly aimed at lower elementary children.
- Star Bright Books (www.starbrightbooks.com) is another website for purchasing bilingual books in both English and 31 other languages. Some books feature text in two different languages on each page. Other titles are written entirely in one language but are also available in other languages. This site is also aimed at lower elementary children.
- The International Children's Digital Library (en.childrenslibrary.org) is a free online source of 4,619 children's books written in 59 languages and at many different levels. This website can supply parents with native language materials to read to their children at home. For teachers, the books can be projected digitally for sharing with whole classes. This website offers English translations of stories from other cultures, not the other way around as is usually the case. That's a plus.
- Bilingual glossaries in at least 38 languages are available for science, social studies, math, and English language arts at steinhardt.nyu.edu/ metrocenter/resources/glossaries. They're also offered for elementary, middle, and high school levels. Glossaries, which don't define the word but simply give its translation, are also a widely accepted testing accommodation for ELLs. I recommend downloading and printing these glossaries to give to ELLs.
- To find out if your state offers the Seal of Biliteracy, visit sealofbiliteracy.org/.

Conclusion

You've learned in this chapter how important it is for ELLs to maintain their home language. This helps students learn English faster and strengthens family and cultural connections, too. In the next chapter, you'll learn that encouraging use of the home language is just one of many ways to help make meaningful connections between home and school.

3

Promoting Family Engagement

MISCONCEPTION: "IMMIGRANT PARENTS JUST AREN'T INVOLVED."

Does the photo in Figure 3.1 of my father reading look like parent engagement to you? I can't recall my father ever reading a book aloud to me or showing much interest in what I was reading on my own, either. That's not very engaged by today's standards, but instead, he was a good reading model himself, and that was more than enough. Watching him relax with a farm magazine every evening showed me that reading was something important that grown-ups did; he didn't have to tell me that. Is it any

FIGURE 3.1 PARENT ENGAGEMENT, CIRCA 1974

wonder, then, that I ended up wanting to read a lot too? This atypical example should also count as family engagement. It certainly counted for me because it connected me to reading. This chapter gives you tips on how to encourage many different kinds of family engagement and how to work together with families of ELLs to help their children.

The Problem with This Misconception

Even though family engagement can mean something different to ELL parents than it does to teachers and other school staff, all forms of family engagement have the same goal—to further student achievement. We shouldn't, therefore, assume parents of ELLs aren't involved simply because they aren't doing what we think indicates parent involvement. That's defining "engagement" too narrowly. The comment that appears at the beginning of this chapter was made during a school staff meeting to explain why a recent fundraiser hadn't been successful. It was, in fact, probably accurate. In a national survey on reported participation in school-related activities, the biggest difference found between English-speaking parents and non-English-speaking parents was in school fundraising: 63 percent of English-speaking parents participated, compared to 32 percent of non-English-speaking parents (Noel, Stark, & Redford, 2016). The real misconception is that fundraising is an effective form of parent engagement.

Research shows that the standard kinds of things we consider to reflect parent involvement (for example, fundraising for the band, serving on the parent–teacher association, and volunteering to help with class parties) are often not closely correlated to student achievement (Goodwin, 2017). In *The Broken Compass: Parental Involvement with Children's Education*, researchers Keith Robinson and Angel Harris (2014) used long-term data from sources such as the National Center for Education Statistics to study this very question. They found that many easily counted forms of parent engagement didn't help student achievement much at all. Types of effective parent involvement, such as reading with children at home or talking with teenagers about college plans, didn't occur at school and so weren't easily observed by teachers. In fact, Noel and colleagues (2016) found that 73 percent of non-English-speaking parents of secondary students, compared to 62 percent of English-speaking parents, reported they expected their children to finish at least four years of college. This shows ELL parents *do* care about their children's education; it's just that they may not be doing the things we assume indicate they care.

ELL parents may also need to support their children's education in different ways because of their financial situations, not necessarily just their language situations. According to Child Trends (n.d.), "Children living in households where a language other than English is spoken are more likely to be poor than are children in English-only households (24 versus 17 percent, in 2016)." ELL parents may be working several different jobs with ever-changing schedules, so it's difficult to do the kinds of things with their children that teachers often recommend. Many barriers to parent involvement, such as lack of time or lack of transportation, affect financially challenged families as well as ELL families. ELL parents I've known welcomed summer school programs, after-school programs, before-school programs, and the like, and they did everything they could to have their children participate in such programs if they were available. I think this shows parents may be more comfortable having their children get help at school. ELL parents may assume teachers are the professionals and we know best. That's not an abdication of responsibility; it shows that parents value our expertise.

Setting This Misconception Straight

I started off titling this chapter "Promoting Parent Engagement," but that's a misconception in itself. Many different kinds of family members, such as siblings, grandparents, aunts, uncles, and cousins, can work together with the school to benefit ELLs. Thinking in terms of only parents is far too narrow. The quote at the beginning of this chapter about immigrant parents not being involved is a misconception because it indicates an incomplete understanding of parent involvement. Parents from many cultures happily give the school authority to do what's best for their children. To them, home and school are separate entities. That's why some of the things we suggest parents do with their children might seem to ELL parents like "the teacher's job." The very idea of a fundraiser might need some explaining before discussing the purpose of a particular fundraiser and asking parents to help with it. Many parents of ELLs didn't attend school in the United States. Imagine how different the U.S. school system must seem to adults who haven't navigated it themselves.

Even if ELL parents want to be involved in their children's education and they understand the rationale behind it, it's often difficult for them to do so due to lack of time, transportation, money, and/or English skills. For example, volunteer requirements like background checks, fingerprinting, and filling out forms ensure student safety, but they also present obstacles to volunteering— even more so for ELL parents than others. If you aren't getting the kind of family support you'd like for additional types of engagement, you might need to do a better job of communicating why such involvement is important and look at ways barriers to such involvement can be eliminated.

Parent Misconceptions

Surprised at some of the misconceptions people have about ELLs? Well, many things about U.S. schools puzzle ELL parents too. Here are some questions that illustrate possible parent misconceptions:

- *Why are U.S. schools so easy?* ELLs with firm academic backgrounds in their native languages may feel some classes—for example, math classes—are easy for them. If a parent asks this question, the student's course placement may be incorrect. You should verify that the student is getting appropriate credit for courses taken at a school outside of the United States. It's important to point out to parents, however, that their children can benefit from support in content classes if they're still learning English. ELL parents might need to be reminded that nowadays "reading" isn't just reading aloud, "writing" isn't just cursive handwriting, and "math" isn't just computation. Anything you can do to explain this shift in focus to ELL parents will help.

- *What happens when my child fails a test?* When parents of ELLs first learn their children's test scores, they want to know what the consequences are. Many ELL parents are familiar with the high-stakes tests common in other countries. What puzzles them about education in the United States is the many different tests and the relatively few consequences attached to any of them, at least for the students. It turns out that ELL parents aren't the only ones confused by the contradictory information they get from test results and report cards. Research commissioned by the nonprofit Learning Heroes (2018) with parents of students in grades 3–8 from a variety of locations and backgrounds showed that nearly 9 in 10 parents believed their child was achieving at or above grade level. Results from the National Assessment of Educational Progress (2017), however, painted a very different picture. Only about one-third of students scored at a proficient level in 2017. ELLs may be receiving passing marks in school subjects but not testing proficient on standardized assessments. When parents learn test results, they'll want to know what happens next and the rationale behind the decision. You, as the classroom teacher, are the best person to answer these questions and address concerns. A good example of this in action is a conference I once attended with the parent of a 3rd grade ELL. I listened, impressed, as the student's teacher clearly informed the parent the child was not reading at grade level. The teacher went on, however, to show evidence of the child's progress toward English proficiency and explained how this process took time. Imagine how pleased we were two years later to report the student had improved enough to be reclassified as a former ELL.

- *Why is it important for my teenager to play sports or participate in clubs?* ELL parents who ask this question often discount the importance of extracurricular activities so popular at the secondary level, such as sports, special interest groups, and service clubs. Parents don't understand that well-rounded students are expected to do things above and beyond getting good grades and high test scores. This emphasis on extracurricular activities can disadvantage students who don't have the time or financial support to participate in them. There is a far too narrow view of what "well-rounded" and "going above and beyond" really mean. Remind parents that working part-time jobs and meeting family responsibilities also count as worthwhile extracurricular activities on college and job applications.

- *What is this career awareness?* Parents of secondary students, especially, may be puzzled by the emphasis on students deciding what they would like to study in college and/or what career they would like to pursue. In many cultures, parents directly advise their children on what they should study. The idea that such an important decision would be made solely by students is not common. In addition, in many countries, admission to higher education is more restricted than it is in the United States. Even after admission, options on what to study and where to study it are limited to students with certain test scores. In contrast, students in the United States have more choice about where and what they want to study after high school. All this choice makes career education not only important but also necessary—for students and their parents!

One encouraging point is that, by and large, ELL parents value teachers' expertise and honor their opinions. Immigrants often come from cultures where teachers are highly respected, and they trust teachers to do the job they're trained to do at school, while they do the job of parenting at home. That may be why ELL parents don't feel the need to make the kind of home-school connections we value, at least for their own sake. It's also why you should explain to parents why you're asking them to do certain things. For example, if you'd like parents to spend time reading with their children at home, pointing out how this leads to better reading achievement might more easily convince them. Hard evidence can convince ELL parents that your suggestions, while undoubtedly culture-based, can work here, in the United States.

Explaining why you're doing something a certain way can also help parents reflect on their own culture-based ideas about education. For example, an ELL parent once suggested I have each student in turn stand up and read a passage out loud in front of the class (probably the way he had been taught in his home country). He listened, though, when I pointed out how having students read in pairs with each other while I circulated throughout the room gave all 25 students much more reading practice. He may have agreed with me at the time just to be polite, but it also didn't hurt that I was later able to show him evidence of his child's improvement. My method was working too!

Another example of evidence convincing skeptical parents comes from a high school math teacher in my district who taught classes heavily populated with 11th graders. The students took a practice ACT at the beginning of the year and then, together with the teacher, analyzed the results and figured out ways they could work on improvement throughout the year in the context of the class coursework. A lot about this practice created buy-in by the students—the pre-test, analyzing the results, figuring out how to make things better, and so on. What created buy-in by the parents, as well, was that the teacher computed the average improvement for the students as a group and posted it on his website. Students knew their individual ACT scores had improved during the course, but anybody looking at the evidence on the website could also see this teacher's methods worked for lots of students.

Working with ELL parents may present some challenges, but there are advantages as well. Parents, in general, often have opinions about what school, assessments, methods, and curriculum should look like based on their experiences in school. What makes ELL parents different from American-born parents is that they have little if any experience attending school in the U.S. system themselves. This may make them more open to new ways of doing things, and that can be a plus for teachers like you who are trying to explain curriculum, assessments, or school policies. For example, when ELL parents see a switch to more nonfiction in the curriculum, a change in how a math problem is explained, or a new assessment being implemented, they are more likely to chalk it up to just one more way that things are done differently here in the United States. In addition, many ELL parents come from countries with education systems far more nationalized than ours, with teacher preparation, curriculum, and assessments all the same throughout the country. The "Common" in the Common Core State Standards makes perfect sense to them.

Making It Right in Your Classroom

- *Rethink homework assignments; in fact, rethink homework, period.* The debate continues over how much and what kind of homework should be assigned or whether it should even be assigned in the first place. If you do give homework, remember that parents shouldn't have to know English to support their children doing it. In fact, no parent should have to do any kind of academic "teaching" at home. Students should have homework they can do independently. ELL parents often say they can't help their children with homework, so don't encourage this kind of opt-out by giving the wrong kind of homework. The fictional homework assignment that follows illustrates the misguided kind of engagement expected of an ELL parent—or any kind of parent, for that matter:

*****

Turkey Habitat
Due Date: Monday, November 18
Project: Diorama

Dear Parents,
We have planned a fun project for November. This project is due Monday, November 18. Each child will research information about turkeys and create a shoebox diorama representing their habitat. Students will be provided with a book to gather facts about their topic. We will also be doing an informational writing piece in class about turkeys to go along with the project. If you are in need of a shoebox or a specific color of paper, please let me know and I will try to provide it. The children will be shown many examples of dioramas, so they should have a good idea of what to do by the time they need to make their own. You can purchase additional craft supplies at Michaels if desired or be creative and use things found around the house. For example, use cotton balls for snow or plastic wrap for ocean water. Your diorama should focus on the habitat of a turkey.

Students will present an oral report and their shoebox to the class. If you have any questions, please let me know. Have fun! I can't wait to see the creativity!

Ms. Stewart

*****

The teacher calls this home assignment a "fun project," but I guarantee this would be far from fun for a parent. Lots of things are wrong with this homework assignment, starting with expecting the parent to go shopping for craft supplies and ending with an exhortation to both parent and student to "be creative." The letter is addressed to parents and starts out talking about the child's assignment, but then in a telling Freudian slip, ends by referring to "your diorama." That may have been unintentional, but it indicates the kind of parent involvement I suggest we reconsider. It puts children with parents who can't help because of language difficulties, job responsibilities, or financial challenges at a disadvantage. Sometimes parent involvement can be something as basic—and important—as getting a well-rested and well-fed child to school every day.

- *Be honest yet encouraging with parents by educating them about the process of English language acquisition.* Often parents don't understand how long it can take for their children to reach full English proficiency. "Fadi, he doing fine?" a parent of a 4th grade ELL once asked during a parent–teacher conference after hearing about her child's class grades and test results. "Well, no," the teacher replied truthfully. She reminded the parent that Fadi was not reading at grade level because he had been in the United States for just three years and his previous schooling had been limited, but she had evidence he was making adequate progress in English.

- *Work* with *parents, not* for *them; talk* with *parents, not* at *them.* Any kind of parent engagement activity needs to pass this test. For example, my school held a series of grade-level "author nights," where students read their writing to an interested audience of parents and other family members. These events drew a high percentage of parents, including ELL parents—until the format changed. Since kindergarteners weren't ready to do an official author night, their teachers decided to hold a gathering where parents could learn how to support their children at home. The attendance was far below the author nights for other grade levels. I have a hunch this was because parents preferred attending events where their children's achievements were highlighted. Also, don't forget to let parents help each other. Some schools outfit a parent resource center, a comfortable gathering place where parents can meet each other and check out books and other materials. One of the most beneficial ELL parent meetings I ever moderated was one I thought I had completely lost control of. Trying to control the meeting was exactly what I was doing wrong. Instead, during the sharing portion of the meeting, parents started asking and answering each other's questions instead of directing them to me. They spoke multiple languages, and we only had an interpreter for Arabic, the most represented language, but their animated back-and-forth in English made me realize parents, in many cases, had greater knowledge of community resources, such as English classes and the like, than I did. After all, they were the ones using them!

- *Realize there may be alternative explanations for what you first assume.* For example, a persistent urban myth among some of my colleagues was that many students who qualified for free or reduced-price lunch came from families who really didn't need it. An observation during a staff meeting once about such students living in nice houses was refuted by a kindergarten teacher's perceptive comment. She had participated in a home visit program for her students and pointed out, "I've been in many of these homes—they may be nice, but there's no furniture inside." The home visit program had given this teacher a more accurate picture of her students' family situations. Similarly, teachers might notice that a student is picked up from school in an expensive car—but not realize an extended family member owns the car, not the student's parents. One might consider Internet access and the accompanying technology a luxury—but it's not for ELL families who want to maintain connections with extended family in their home countries.

- *Many report cards and test reports are difficult to understand, but recognize the problem is with the papers not the parents.* Keep all written communication simple. Many teachers think if they can just get everything translated, the problem will be solved. Even if it were possible, many class newsletters and the like still wouldn't be comprehensible because they're often written badly to begin with. Here's a fictional example of a standard teacher introduction letter to parents. See if you can identify the common weaknesses in it:

*****

August 2019

Dear Parents and Students,

Welcome to fifth grade!!! I am so excited to have you in my class this year. My goal is your success. I expect hard work, as I have high expectations for you. My name is Joyce Noname. I am originally from Omaha, Nebraska, and our family loves the Nebraska Cornhuskers!! I received my bachelor's degree in Elementary Education from the University of Nebraska and my master's degree in Curriculum and Instruction from the University of Kansas. I have taught kindergarten through sixth grade and I LOVE it!

I am married to a wonderful husband, Bob Noname, and we have two fabulous daughters. Samantha Elizabeth is in the seventh grade at John Middle School. Regina Grace is in the fourth grade here at B. G. Commons. I love to spend time with my family and I love to read!

Fifth grade is my absolute favorite grade to teach! I love, Love, LOVE reading! I am excited about introducing your child to a number of great books this year. I am excited to meet and get to know each of you! I have experience and a long-held passion for teaching and learning. Each child grows and changes so much at this time in their lives; I cannot wait to see what great things this year has in store for your children! I firmly believe that in order for your child to have the best year possible, we must work together to create a team. By being a teacher, as well as having two daughters in school, I know the importance of a good working relationship between a parent and a teacher. Communication is extremely important, and I am here to answer any questions that you might have regarding your child or the curriculum. Always feel free to contact me with any questions or concerns you or your child might have.

I am looking forward to an AWESOME year! Thank you for your time.

Joyce Noname

*****

This letter of introduction combines several elements of poorly written parent communication:

- *Lack of clear audience.* The teacher starts out by saying she's excited to "have you in my class," but she addresses the letter to both the parents and the students. Then she goes on to talk about "your child." This mistake is easier to make for upper-grade teachers because their students can actually read and understand written communication. In this example, though, 5th grade students and their parents would have quite different questions and concerns about the coming school year. A separate letter to each of these audiences would be easier for everybody to understand.
- *Overly casual tone.* The teacher wants to sound enthusiastic about the coming school year, but the punctuation and word choice (for example, LOVE!, AWESOME!, fabulous) just make it look like a middle school student wrote the letter.
- *Unsubstantiated clichés.* "I have experience and a long-held passion for teaching and learning." "We must work together to create a team." "I expect hard work."

- *Too much irrelevant information.* "Wonderful husband," "fabulous daughters," "our family loves the Nebraska Cornhuskers."
- *Missing contact information.* The teacher says "feel free to contact me" but doesn't give parents concrete contact information.

Following is a rewrite at half the length with the same essential information:

* * * * *

August 2019

Dear Parents,

My name is Joyce Noname, and I am excited to have your child in my class this year. I am originally from Omaha, Nebraska. I received my bachelor's degree in elementary education from the University of Nebraska and my master's degree in curriculum and instruction from the University of Kansas. I have taught kindergarten through sixth grade, but my favorite grade is fifth grade. I am married to Bob Noname, and we have two daughters. Samantha Elizabeth is a seventh grader at John Middle School, and Regina Grace is in the fourth grade here at B. G. Commons. I love reading and spending time with my family.

I am eager to meet you and begin building a good working relationship. I am here to answer any questions you may have. Feel free to contact me at 386-943-2285 or joycenoname@gmail.com. I look forward to a great year!

Joyce Noname

* * * * *

This shorter version is easier to read because it's in simple English. Conveniently, that would also make it easier to translate into other languages. Do a favor for the parents of all your students—ELL as well as non-ELL—and use clear English in your written communication. Try to use positive, inclusive language when speaking too. Figure 3.2 illustrates poor language choices and alternative wording that could be used both in parent communications and when you are speaking with colleagues about your students and their families. Notice that the alternative wording puts the focus on the student not the teacher.

FIGURE 3.2 WATCH YOUR LANGUAGE!

Instead of saying this:	Say this:
Kiddos	Students
My kids	My students
I just love having Fadi in my class!	Fadi is a well-behaved student who follows directions.
I think Mariam is such a sweet little girl.	Mariam is a well-behaved student who has many friends in class.
Does he work for you?	Does he do his work in your class?
He doesn't do my homework.	He doesn't do his homework.
My class.	Algebra II, English I, Food Science, and so on
Those people	Our students' parents
He can't _____.	He can _____.
Mrs. Yousif can't speak English.	Mrs. Yousif speaks Arabic.
My curriculum	The curriculum
Do you have any questions?	Ask me a question.
Do you understand?	What was the hardest thing to understand? Why?

A LITTLE EXTRA . . .

- I highly recommend ¡Colorín Colorado! (www.colorincolorado.org), a website for everything about ELLs. I especially like the reading tip sheets for parents in 13 languages (www.colorincolorado.org/reading-tip-sheets-parents). I recommend printing and distributing them at parent–teacher conferences.
- Unite for Literacy (www.uniteforliteracy.com) offers home reading practice with a variety of basic-level nonfiction books printed in English. Audio narration is available in English and in 41 other languages.

Conclusion

ELL parents *do* care about their children's education—they just may demonstrate their caring in ways that are unfamiliar to you. Be willing to adjust your perceptions of what effective parent engagement is and be ready to fully explain to parents what you think it looks like. It's not necessarily *how much*, but *how* parents are involved. In the next chapter, we'll look at how you can meet the needs of ELLs who probably concern you the most—newcomers.

You *Can* Teach Newcomers—Foundational Principles for Instruction

MISCONCEPTION: "HOW DO YOU TEACH THEM IF YOU CAN'T SPEAK THEIR LANGUAGE?"

"I feel like the world's worst teacher," one of my colleagues once remarked as we were discussing how to meet the needs of her newcomers. Newcomers in your classes might make you feel that way too. It seems like these ELLs need everything and what we can do is never enough. A great way to start would be having the ability to speak the native languages of all our ELLs, but that's not possible unless you're a polyglot. The people asking me the question that appears at the beginning of this chapter are assuming the only way to successfully teach ELL newcomers is to speak their home languages. It's one way, but it's not the only way. This chapter will show you how to make your instruction comprehensible to beginning ELLs even if you don't speak their languages.

The Problem with This Misconception

The misconception in this chapter is actually rooted in some valid research. A large meta-analysis of various program models for ELLs showed bilingual instruction does benefit students (Lindholm-Leary & Borsato, 2006). In the short term, younger students in bilingual programs had lower achievement levels compared with their ELL or non-English-speaking peers, but in the long term, older students who had spent more time in bilingual programs were able to catch up to, and even surpass, the achievement levels of their peers. As in most situations, much depended on the quality of such programs and the length of time students spent in them. Much also depends on how bilingual education is defined. For example, my own school district had a "bilingual education" department for years, but content was never taught in two languages. I once applied for a "bilingual/reading teacher" job opening and realized at the interview that what the principal really wanted was a teacher of English as a second language. I wasn't bilingual in any of the students' languages, but I got the job. My principal might have had a more qualified applicant pool, however, if he'd had a better understanding of the terms he was using in the job announcement.

It *is* helpful to speak your students' home languages, but that by itself does not determine your students' academic progress. Good bilingual programs may be the gold standard for helping ELLs reach academic proficiency in two languages, but they're not yet a practical reality for most schools in the United States because of the shortage of qualified teachers and appropriate teaching materials. Bilingual programs are also difficult to implement in super-diverse schools with students from many different language backgrounds, not just one. I've been asked many times over the years, "How many languages do you speak?" and, unfortunately, my answer has had to be, "None very well." It's helpful if language acquisition specialists speak one of their students' home languages, but it's not required. You can't assume, for example, that an ESL teacher speaks Spanish; what you *can* assume, however, is language acquisition specialists have training in how to teach all ELLs, no matter what language they speak at home. That helps. I've also lived in another country and directly experienced learning a new language from scratch, albeit with far more advantages (maturity, education, and financial security, just to name a few) than the newcomers in your class have. That experience helped me. Experience living abroad and/or learning another language will help you too, if you have it. In the meantime, ELLs, even newcomers, will spend much of their school day in general education classrooms. Real learning needs to continue there as well—in any language.

Setting This Misconception Straight

Newcomers *do* belong in your classroom, and they *can* learn there too. The U.S. Department of Education (2016) instructs schools to "ensure that EL students have equal opportunities to meaningfully participate in all curricular and extracurricular activities" (p. 6). An English language acquisition specialist will spend more time with newcomers than other ELLs, but that doesn't mean general education teachers aren't responsible for teaching them too. Your job as a classroom teacher is to figure out how to best help newcomers and use the support your school has. Many different models can adequately support ELLs because these students and the schools they attend are so different. I should know. I taught in my district's newcomer program for elementary students for seven years and worried when my district disbanded it in favor of school-based ESL support. I was sure newcomer ELLs would suffer because they would be spending much less time in specialized classes. To my surprise, data collected in the ensuing years showed that newcomers made as much progress in the school-based model as they had in the newcomer program. Even better, intermediate- and higher-level ELLs were receiving more support because an ESL teacher was now based in each of our district's elementary schools. This shows that evidence of achievement is a good way to determine which model works best. An elementary school with 10 or fewer newcomers might meet their needs with a bilingual paraprofessional who works with them for 30 minutes each day; a district with many newcomers might create a magnet program for high school newcomers who need specialized instruction for a year or less. According to a recent Every Student Succeeds Act (ESSA) guidance document, some of the more relevant federal mandates for programs are that they (1) be based on sound educational theory, (2) have resources and personnel to carry out the program effectively, and (3) produce results in a reasonable amount of time (U.S. Department of Education, 2016). Districts may set requirements for themselves; the federal government actually leaves a lot of discretion up to individual districts. What's the same everywhere is that newcomers in your classrooms can and will learn if you provide appropriate supports. The rest of this chapter will help you provide those supports.

Making It Right in Your Classroom

The socioemotional challenges your newcomers may be facing are certainly not unique. Students from other kinds of disadvantaged backgrounds also struggle with these challenges. They're not easily fixed either, so "making it right in your classroom" is probably not possible in the short term. Still, you should be aware of issues newcomers may be dealing with and understand the ways those obstacles might differ from the ones other students face:

• *Financial issues.* ELLs in general are more likely than other students to be economically disadvantaged. It's even more likely with students whose families are new to the United States. Newcomer families may be living temporarily with extended family members until they get financial footing. That may be a source of comfort, but it can also lead to stress. Newcomers may still worry about family members remaining in their home countries and/or feel obligated to send money to relatives left behind. Newcomer families who had solid financial footing in their home countries will still probably experience temporary financial insecurity after arriving in the United States. Even if ELL parents had professional credentials and education in the home country, these don't easily transfer to equivalent job status in a new country. Newcomers, even more than other ELLs, may not have funds for field trips, band instruments, school supplies, outerwear, and the like.

- *Incomplete academic history.* It's difficult to get good information for new students, even if they're transferring from another school in the United States. It's even more difficult with ELL newcomers who may have school records that are difficult to understand even when they're available. Be careful not to underestimate your newcomers—they may have grade-level skills, but they can't yet demonstrate them in English. Newcomers may worry that their teachers will assume their knowledge is limited because their English is limited. At the same time, there may be good reasons for missing skills. For example, newcomers may have been out of school for extended periods. That means the 2nd grader in your class might be having difficulties with a craft project because he's not had much experience using scissors and glue. A middle school newcomer might be surprised to learn the Earth is round simply because she was out of school for several years and missed gaining lots of general world knowledge.

- *Ambivalence about being here.* Iraqi newcomers in my area of metro Detroit, Michigan, were "pulled" to America for many years for education and economic reasons. Later, as refugees, they were "pushed" into the United States because of turmoil in their home country. Immigrant parents and ELLs old enough to remember have told me that while they appreciate what they have in the United States, what they really wish for is their life back in their home countries without the economic hardships, threats of violence, and political upheavals that forced them to come to the United States in the first place. Your students and their parents may also be experiencing similar feelings of loss and displacement.

- *Trauma and parents' related safety concerns.* Your newcomers may have experienced violence such as kidnappings of family members, arson, or other kinds of trauma. This is why it would be perfectly logical for parents to worry until they realize their children are safe here. This may play out with parents seeming to be overly concerned about putting students on buses to go to school, sending students on field trips, and the like.

- *Different social skills or gaps in social skills.* Newcomers may have been under firm external control in schools in their home countries, so they haven't developed as much internal discipline as their classmates. Newcomers will most likely respect and expect firmness. But to learn to do the right thing when nobody's watching, they'll have to understand the rules first. Students may need to be shown how to line up in the hallway, how to play appropriately at recess, how to eat lunch in the cafeteria, and so on. When teaching newcomers in Michigan, I even demonstrated how to play in the snow at recess. ("Yes, you can build a snowman, and I'll show you how, but no, you can't throw snowballs.") A rule in every school is to keep hands and feet to yourself, but many newcomer students want to hug everybody they like at inappropriate times and hit everybody they don't like. Newcomers and even their parents may not realize at first that aggressive language ("I kill you!") and/or aggressive behavior (pretend gunplay, for example) are no-nos in American schools. Fortunately, as newcomers become more proficient with the nuances of social English, they'll be able to negotiate meaning and communicate feelings more accurately. For example, "I kill you!" during a soccer game at recess will become "You fouled!" In the cafeteria, "I love you, honey" will become "Can I eat lunch with you?" General education classmates of newcomers will also model appropriate behaviors.

Each part of a newcomer's typical school day presents both challenges as well as opportunities, as shown in Figure 4.1.

FIGURE 4.1 A NEWCOMER'S SCHOOL DAY: CHALLENGES AND OPPORTUNITIES

A Newcomer's School Day	Challenge	Opportunity
Ride to school on the bus	Bus schedules and pick-up and drop-off locations can be very confusing for newcomer families. If a newcomer misses the bus, other transportation options are often not available.	Students can learn and practice social English.
Greet the teacher	Students new to U.S. school culture may address their teachers as "Miss" or "Teacher."	Students can learn the appropriate way to address their teachers—for example, Mr. Jones, Ms. Popovich, or Mrs. Cushard.
Recess (for elementary students)	Newcomers may not be familiar with games their classmates like to play, such as basketball or American football.	Students can learn and practice social English. English ability is less of a concern when playing games and doing other activities.
Breakfast and lunch	What in the world is an "ultimate breakfast bar," a "Bosco stick," or an "Italian dunker"? Descriptions of menu items are hard to understand, even for native speakers of English.	Breakfast and lunch offer tangible opportunities for helpful kitchen staff to answer students' questions about food. Students will learn what menu item descriptions mean the first time they eat these items. The school cafeteria is also a great place to make friends and practice social English.
Language arts	At both the secondary and elementary levels, this is typically the part of the school day when newcomers are receiving specialized instruction in separate courses or pull-out sessions with ESL professionals. This means that, inevitably, newcomers are missing something.	In smaller groups and special classes, newcomers usually feel more comfortable asking questions and practicing English. Their teachers are specially trained in English language development.

(CONTINUES)

FIGURE 4.1 A NEWCOMER'S SCHOOL DAY:
CHALLENGES AND OPPORTUNITIES (CONTINUED)

A Newcomer's School Day	Challenge	Opportunity
Math	Students and their parents may be unpleasantly surprised by how much English is necessary to do math.	Numbers may be something familiar and reassuring from past schoolwork.
Social studies	This area has a higher reading load and is more text dependent. Content is also more culture bound. For example, no newcomers in a North Carolina classroom will have studied North Carolina history in their home countries.	Much of the content taught in social studies classes may appear later in the exams students and their family members will be taking for U.S. citizenship. What a great example of relevance!
Science	Reading materials will need to be adapted. Students may have difficulty understanding information presented in lecture format without any demonstrations or visuals.	Experiments and other lab activities offer hands-on opportunities. Science is less culture based, so newcomers' prior science knowledge will transfer more easily.
Elective courses: music, physical education, vocational education, and so on	At the secondary level, newcomers and their parents may not understand the importance of elective courses.	These courses offer learning by doing. Hands-on activities help make content accessible for ELLs.

You'll find tips in later chapters on how to make your instruction comprehensible for ELLs at all ability levels. Here, though, are some easy ways to make life easier for your newcomers and for you too:

• *Find out what your new ELLs know.* A language-free calculation test can show a student's math ability, at least at elementary levels. I've learned, however, that students can sometimes misunderstand how problems are presented even on a language-free assessment, so this might not necessarily tell you everything your students know. If your students have attended school in their home countries, ask them to read you something in their native languages. That's another good reason for your school to have a supply of bilingual books in various languages on hand. For example, when I asked a 5th grade newcomer from Vietnam to read a Vietnamese picture book aloud to me, she did so in what sounded to me like fluent Vietnamese. I wasn't sure because I didn't know Vietnamese, but still, it told me something. When the student was also able to produce a writing sample in Vietnamese, I learned even more. Get a writing sample in English by asking students to write about themselves. If that's not possible, ask them to write something in their native languages, or if you want to go the totally nonverbal route, have them write about a picture. You'll discover that newcomers with previous schooling in their home countries are proud to show their classroom teachers what they know—in English and in their native languages. This is important information for teachers because, as you learned in Chapter 2, a student's native language literacy skills can transfer and make learning a second language easier. Your school's language acquisition specialist will also do more formal English proficiency screening and other assessments—don't be shy about asking for this information. You need it too.

• *Simplify your speech.* It's not always a matter of slowing down or talking more loudly. It's better to ask a student, "What did you eat for lunch?" at a normal speaking rate than to say slowly, "I bet you didn't like the mystery meat in the cafeteria today, did you?" The first question is a direct question and relatively easy to answer. The second is a negative question, or so-called tag question, notoriously difficult for ELLs to understand. It also contains slang expressions ("I bet" and "mystery meat").

Speaking at a normal rate makes your intonation more natural and easier to understand. Avoid adopting sing-song intonation or using stunted expressions; it won't make you more comprehensible. Watch out for puns, slang, or plays on words that would be difficult for newcomers to understand. If you post clever messages in your classroom, discussing the word play with students would be a good teaching opportunity. All the following examples, however, were found in school hallways where they might confuse ELL parents and other visitors:

—"Writing Is Snow Much Fun!" (Seeing "snow" substituted for "so" over this hallway display of student writing might perplex somebody who is new to English.)

—"Donut Worry. Do Your Best!" (This motivational sign, showing a picture of a donut, was posted in the school hallway during state assessments.)

—"A Toast to the New Year!" (This sign, which included a picture of a toaster, was posted above students' New Year's resolutions. It's probably just as well elementary ELLs didn't understand the other, less appropriate, meaning of "a toast.")

It's not necessary to change everything you put on the wall, but using more direct English will help all your parents and students better understand what you're trying to communicate.

• *Be careful about using parodies before students know the original version.* Students at the school where I taught newcomers presented a play every year for the entire student body. Often it was a parody of an original story—an adapted *Little Red Riding Hood*, for example, or a different take on *The Wizard of Oz*. There was nothing particularly wrong with this since comparing two versions of a story involves higher-order thinking. I did, however, need to make sure my newcomers knew the original story first before watching the adapted version. As another example, every year at Thanksgiving, teachers at my school have students do clever projects like disguising a paper turkey or writing creative stories encouraging people to eat something besides turkey or describing how to cook a turkey. Ironically, many students never learn about *real* turkeys. Third grade ELLs still routinely refer to them as chickens, even though they've done Thanksgiving activities since kindergarten.

- *Don't assume cultural background knowledge.* "Which team will you be rooting for in the Super Bowl?" a colleague once asked a newcomer. Credit the teacher for reaching out, but what seemed like a good way to start a conversation with this student ended up being a conversation stopper instead. Like a fish that doesn't think much about being in water, the teacher didn't realize newcomers might not know about American football, let alone which teams were playing in the Super Bowl. A similar example is a Christmas-around-the-world project teachers did with their students every December at a school where I once worked. The activity was intended to be inclusive, but, in fact, the teachers were forgetting that half of the world's population, and undoubtedly some of the students in their classes, didn't observe Christmas.

- *Don't insist on a lot of spoken English at first.* Teachers sometimes take it personally when newcomers won't (because they can't!) make small talk with them, respond to greetings, participate in class discussions, and the like. As ELLs begin learning English, they often understand more than they can speak. In fact, the productive domains of English, speaking and writing, almost always develop more slowly than the receptive domains, listening and reading, throughout the entire process of reaching English proficiency. For example, on the WIDA ACCESS for ELLs 2.0, the annual English language proficiency test used by my state of Michigan and many other states, ELLs had a mean listening score of 5 ("bridging") on a six-point scale. In contrast, the mean speaking score was nearly two levels lower—3.1 ("developing"). Listening had the highest mean score of all the domains for the previous five years as well (Michigan Center for Educational Performance and Information, 2018). There's no reason to believe this would be different for ELLs in other parts of the United States.

- *Realize that first names can confuse new speakers of English.* It can be difficult for ELLs to tell the gender of a name. How in the world would anyone know, unless they had lots of cultural background knowledge, that Autumn is a girl's name and Pierce is a boy's name? Nicknames are also troublesome. They can even confuse grown-up nonnative speakers of English like my husband. "Is Buster a name people give their kids?" he asked me as he was writing a check for someone who had done repair work at our house. My husband knew Buster was a male name because he had met the person, but he had no idea whether Buster was a "real" given name or a nickname. The only Buster he knew was our neighbor's dog! Conversely, your ELLs' names may flummox you. Learn to pronounce their names correctly and resist the urge to give them an "American name" like the teacher in Chapter 1 who wanted to change the Turkish spelling of little Can's name to John. Getting names right is one easy way to begin connecting with your ELLs.

- *Watch out for "word vomit" in your classroom.* It's good to write things down for ELLs but putting *everything* on the walls is just as confusing. The information on the classroom wall in Figure 4.2 would be hard to decipher even for a literate adult. For an ELL, it might as well be Egyptian hieroglyphics. Even if a person were literate in hieroglyphics, the meaning of everything on the whiteboard in the image would be tough to figure out because there's just too much print everywhere. Excessive visual stimulation, in fact, can hamper learning for all students, not just ELLs. Several researchers had groups of students do tasks in different environments and found they did better in a less-stimulating environment (Rodrigues & Pandeirada, 2018). They recommend that at least 20–50 percent of the wall space in a classroom should be free. Is this true for your classroom?

FIGURE 4.2 WORD VOMIT

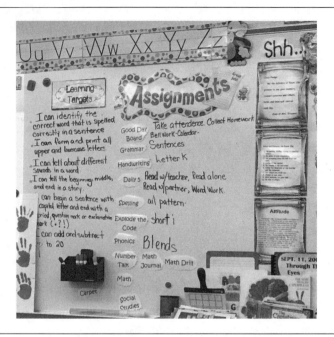

- *Don't use cursive.* A 5th grade newcomer preparing to leave elementary school once asked me to "translate" her memory book. Her teachers had written lovely messages to this student, but she couldn't read them because they were in cursive. Using manuscript writing would have allowed this student to directly read, and remember, what her teachers had said. Avoiding cursive when writing on students' papers, on the board, and the like is one of the easiest ways you can make your written communication accessible to ELLs. The value of teaching students cursive continues to be debated, but the increased use of technology for writing will eventually make this a moot point. I don't see the value in using instructional time for teaching cursive myself, but if you think it's important, please don't *require* your ELLs to use cursive when they write. Otherwise, students are likely to spend too much time worrying about how to make a capital G in cursive, for example, and not enough time thinking about how and what they're going to write.

- *Use a laser pointer to highlight visuals.* A pointer allows you to easily guide your students' eyes to pertinent information in a visual. A laser pointer also lets you point to things in your classroom you wouldn't be able to touch otherwise. If nothing else, using a laser pointer keeps your hands and body away from the visual, making them less distracting for viewers.

- *Use captions on video clips.* You'll need to check first to see if the captions are good. (You *are* previewing the video clips you show your students, aren't you?) Some captions are so bad they're not worth it. The good captions, though, are helpful, and research shows that supports, such as captioning, help ELLs improve (What Works Clearinghouse, 2013). Use them as much as you can. This is an example of something really easy you can do to make your instruction more accessible.

- *Have procedures in place to easily add students to your classroom.* Newcomers can enroll at any time of the year, sometimes without much advance notice. That's not convenient, but just in case, be sure you can welcome a new student at the drop of a hat at any time during the year. One of my teaching colleagues always had an extra desk in his classroom with materials a new student would need. When a new student did indeed enroll, everything was ready with no last-minute scrambling for supplies or running to the copy machine. It made the new student feel welcomed rather than a bother.

- *Work with your language acquisition specialist to help your newcomers.* Make a plan in consultation with this specialist, keeping in mind that no single arrangement is best for every student. If you and your specialist decide newcomers should leave your classroom for support, realize this will more than make up for anything they might be "missing." Communicate with your specialist about what's happening in your classroom. That way your newcomers can get the kind of support when they're out of your classroom that will help them when they return. As a language acquisition specialist myself, I always found it helpful to know what themes were being covered, what texts were being used, and what activities were being planned. I could then preview with newcomers to get them ready for instruction and also follow up to ensure they understood.

- *Read aloud—you as well as your students.* Picture books, especially, can be helpful to newcomers of all ages. "Read aloud to your students every day—even three times a day!" my sister, a master kindergarten teacher, advised me when I began teaching an elementary self-contained class for newcomers. She was right; reading aloud to my newcomers turned out to be one of the best ways to develop their English ability. Later, as a school-based language acquisition teacher, I continued to read aloud to students in small group sessions and encouraged my general education colleagues to do so too. Listening to a teacher read aloud a picture book and then having the chance to discuss it afterward, page by page, is one of the most valuable things young ELLs can do. Reading aloud to older ELLs also brings benefits. Teachers can use both fiction and nonfiction picture books to introduce students to a variety of genres, highlight specific reading strategies, and build content knowledge in science and social studies.

  One of my colleagues uses an effective, ELL-friendly, read-aloud routine with her 4th graders. Because she uses picture books, her routine is accessible to newcomers; and because it gives students practice in the four language domains—listening, speaking, reading, and writing—it helps ELLs at all levels improve. Even better, she often uses additional visual support, like a video read-aloud of the same book (but for a different purpose), a related video clip, or images. After students listen to the book and have a chance to talk about it with their classmates, they write about it in their reading response notebooks.

The teacher models writing the responses at the beginning of the year and then gradually releases responsibility to the students. I often saw students using their notebooks to make connections about authors and/or books: "Oh, we read a book by Eve Bunting before!" The responses in Figure 4.3 were written by the same 4th grade ELL just a few months apart. This student's improvement reminds all of us, even teachers of older students, that reading aloud gets results.

FIGURE 4.3 READING LOG SAMPLE DEMONSTRATING STUDENT IMPROVEMENT IN JUST MONTHS

December 2	Several months later
Wanda wanda what to get the. Kite and that sad no and she was. Cep wining rot ran tray son fin you can cep. It than she cep it.	First they had a red Balloon and it was a hart for his dad the they want for the ship to give the Balloon then their were so much people and they had ballons to give to there family and they saw the big ship and the littal boy bat the balloon flyed up and my and the dad cam back.

- *Secondary teachers, make sure your newcomers get credit for their previous study, if any.* You probably won't be involved with registering a student, but if a student tells you a course is easy, he may have studied it before in the home country. Sometimes capable ELLs aren't given access to appropriate courses simply because of their English proficiency and instead are tracked into developmental courses. As I've pointed out before, ELLs' native language education has a big influence on how easily they can learn concepts in a new language. For example, the success in 9th grade of a Spanish-speaking student who has completed one year of 8th grade in the United States depends just as much on the student's academic preparation in his home country as it does his English ability. Whether a newcomer from Bangladesh, for example, can succeed in a biology class depends as much on her knowledge of science from education in her home country as it does on her English ability. The gap for secondary newcomers is so much greater than for elementary newcomers, but secondary ELLs with literacy in their native language have much more to build upon than young ELLs with no first-language literacy. Use this native language literacy—it's a strength.

A LITTLE EXTRA . . .

- *Immersion* (www.immersionfilm.com) is a powerful 12-minute film that highlights some of the difficulties encountered by newcomers. It follows a young Spanish-speaking boy in his home and school and shows viewers what it's like to be a newcomer faced with playground teasing and incomprehensible state assessments. His helpful teacher is handcuffed by testing requirements that limit the use of accommodations and other native language support. Watch the film to identify the issues you think are most relevant to your situation.

- *The Newcomers: Finding Refuge, Friendship, and Hope in an American Classroom* follows a classroom of newcomers in a high school in Denver, Colorado. Author Helen Thorpe, a journalist and former first lady of Colorado, embedded herself in a high school newcomer class for a year. Her observations, coming from a noneducator, are illuminating for teachers.

Conclusion

ELLs, including newcomers, have a legal right to access the core curriculum. They need to be in your general education classes. The question at the beginning of this chapter—asking how I could teach ELLs without knowing their languages—was focusing on what I couldn't do. I couldn't speak Arabic, I couldn't speak

Spanish, I couldn't speak Albanian, and so on. Misconceptions like that sell teachers and ELLs short. Newcomers *can* learn in your classes, and I hope this chapter has shown you how you *can* successfully teach them. From my experience, teachers tend to overestimate newcomer ELLs' background knowledge and preparation—but underestimate what they can do with appropriate supports. Chapter 5 will describe such supports for various content areas.

You *Can* Teach Newcomers—Ideas for Instruction Across the Content Areas

MISCONCEPTION: "ELLs ARE USUALLY GOOD IN MATH."

Teachers in content areas often assume newcomers will learn English in their specialized classes. That's correct, but to reach proficiency as soon as possible, newcomers also need to be taught English *through* content. In this chapter, you'll get tips for helping newcomers make the most of the time they spend in your content classes, learning all of the other subjects as well as English.

The Problem with This Misconception

The quote at the beginning of this chapter (a statement made by a general education teacher) illustrates a positive stereotype I wish were more often true. Yes, many of our luckier foreign-born students come to us with solid academic backgrounds in their native languages, and these students may have studied more advanced math than what they encounter in American schools. The language demands of math nowadays, however, can make it difficult for even well-prepared ELLs. Math materials today use much more text, even beyond the traditional word problems. I sometimes show parents and students an old math textbook full of computation exercises and then a newer math textbook with many word problems. It's easy then to visually understand that math isn't just numbers anymore. In addition, students are expected to speak and write about how they solved math problems, using math talks and math journals. These extra language demands make math instruction much richer, but they also can make math more difficult for ELLs—more difficult than they or you would expect—even if they know the calculations required to solve problems. An ELL with basic English proficiency but with a strong grounding in math will still need some language support in a mainstream math class. An ELL who has had interrupted or limited schooling will need even more support.

Setting This Misconception Straight

One good thing for math teachers is that, even though the content nowadays is awash in English, ELLs will more likely be comfortable in your math class because of their familiarity with numbers. Students with a solid math background are in the best situation of all—they have the opportunity to learn the English of math while reviewing content and concepts they already know in their native languages. Science, technology, engineering, and math (STEM) fields and careers carry high prestige in many countries, even more so than in the United States, so this can be an advantage as well. Finally, math is an area in which students get most of their instruction in school, not at home, so it's less susceptible to environmental factors that might adversely affect other subjects, such as reading. That means if you're teaching math, you have an opportunity to make a big difference!

Making It Right in Your Classroom: Math

Assessing what a newcomer already knows is your highest priority so that you can begin appropriate instruction as soon as possible. Find a screener or other simple assessment that tells you how much your ELLs understand basic math concepts. With newcomers, I've used a math assessment that covered just calculation. I thought students would know Arabic numbers like the ones used in the United States, and most of them did. I was surprised, though, to discover that some Arabic-speaking students used different Eastern Arabic numerals. Perkins and Flores (2002) confirm what I noticed and cite even more examples of different kinds of mathematical notation systems and procedures. Proper placement is a challenge with transient students entering school throughout the school year, but it's essential. Don't be like the teacher who had a newcomer playing math games at the computer while the rest of the class was doing a math lesson simply because she assumed low English proficiency meant low math skills. Assessing this newcomer's skills would have shown otherwise.

For older newcomers, it's important to review their previous academic credentials so that placement is done accurately. Timely English proficiency screening is especially important at the secondary level because there's less time to catch up and get credit. Correct course placement, then, is critical. You don't want capable ELLs placed in classes they don't need. Studies already show ELLs are less likely to be considered for advanced coursework, such as AP courses. They are also less likely to have access to core content classes leading to a timely high school graduation and an opportunity for postsecondary education (Umansky et al., 2016).

If you use ability groups for math, as many elementary teachers already do for reading, make sure these groupings remain flexible. Keeping the same groupings for other subjects is a bad practice for all students, but ELLs may have especially wide variation in their skill levels. A newcomer may mistakenly be placed in a low math group based on assessments that are really measuring language, not math.

Word problems pose difficulties for beginning ELLs because they require the student to read and understand a passage. The language keeps ELLs from being able to demonstrate all of their math knowledge. The money and measurement systems used in the United States will probably also be new to ELLs. In addition, many word problems use confusing names and assume cultural background knowledge. Here's an example:

> Tre scored 117 points this season. He scored all of his points with 50-yard field goal kicks. Each field goal is worth three points. He played in 13 games, and he scored the same number of points in each game. How many field goals did Tre make in each game?

The math required to solve this problem is straightforward, and the problem does tell the student a field goal is worth three points. Still, a student unfamiliar with American football might have difficulty contextualizing what is intended to be an authentic math problem. It *is* authentic—if you're a football fan.

Figure 5.1 shows another example of how we can make it hard for newcomers to show their knowledge. The newcomer who asked me about an assignment similar to this fictional example understood how to plot coordinates on a grid map. I knew because she had put her first name, her school's name, her favorite color, and her last name in the correct grids. What was stumping her was that, even though she could sound out and read the words, she didn't know what cleats or a goal post or goggles looked like. I drew pictures by the words, and the student easily completed the worksheet. The second part of the worksheet used real-life examples like the student's first name, making it easier for the student to demonstrate the relevant math skill. Whenever possible, try to use real-life examples that are meaningful to students. This could involve

FIGURE 5.1 PLOTTING COORDINATES ON A GRID MAP: WHAT IS BEING ASSESSED?

	1	2	3	4
A	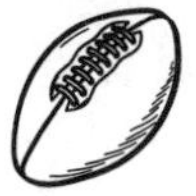		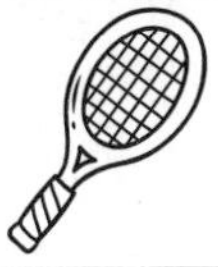	
B		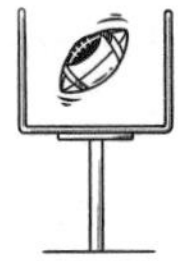		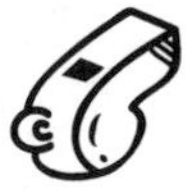
C	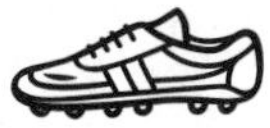		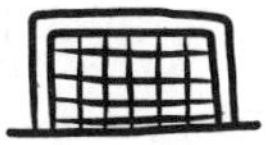	
D		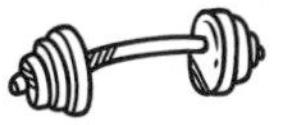		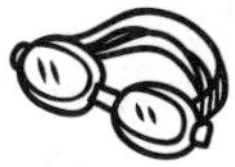

Identify the grid box location for the following items.

1.______ barbell

2.______ cleats

3.______ football

4.______ whistle

5.______ tennis racket

6.______ hockey goal net

7.______ swimming goggles

8.______ goal post

Fill in these grid boxes with your . . .

A-2 first name **D-1 favorite color**

C-4 school's name **B-3 last name**

something like counting donated items for a school food drive or having students draw graphs to chart their progress on a skill.

Students should "do" math using all four English domains—listening, speaking, reading, and writing. It's not enough for students just to find the answer; they should also be able to talk and write about how they found it. They need to learn math, but they also need to learn how to use the language of math through math talks and math journaling. The move to Common Core State Standards in math is a positive one for newcomers, mainly because under Common Core, fewer math concepts are covered in more depth (Common Core State Standards Initiative, 2019b). This recycling and building on past knowledge is good for all students but especially for new ELLs. The Common Core math standards also emphasize analyzing math answers—with less emphasis on the correct answer and more focus on problem-solving techniques. This is good for ELLs because it involves all four English domains.

Making It Right in Your Classroom: Language Arts

Too often, reading instruction in the elementary language arts block is focused on skill building to the detriment of building knowledge about a topic. I want to cry when I ask students, "What are you studying?" and they respond "fluency" or, even worse, "page 72." Teaching thematically in the language arts block can do double duty by helping students learn about a single topic through listening, speaking, reading, and writing. It can also increase engagement because students are *learning something* (the whole point of reading), not simply doing "work." Thematic teaching should be easier to implement at the secondary level. At the very least, when students walk into a high school chemistry classroom, they're reasonably sure they'll be studying chemistry. With language arts, the topics can be all over the place. If you're lucky enough to have materials coordinated by theme, then use them, or at least try. I once watched an elementary teacher do a read-aloud about Groundhog Day—on Halloween. That's not trying. By contrast, another colleague always seemed to be able to coordinate her teaching materials by theme. When I asked her how she did it, she had a simple answer: "I follow our district's pacing guides." Our district's curriculum department had taken pains to coordinate themes linking language arts, social studies, and science, but when teachers strayed far from the pacing guides, their students lost the benefits of this advance planning.

This Will Likely Work

For a month-long social studies unit on Native Americans in Michigan, 3rd grade students also got a lot of language arts practice by doing activities that included all the language domains—listening, speaking, reading, and writing. Students built models of Native American villages and listened to a speaker who showed them Native American artifacts. The teacher also used selected video clips and articles at various reading levels to help all students learn about the topic. The teacher worried she was "beating the topic to death," but because she was teaching thematically, she was making it easier for all students to learn the information. She was also helping her ELLs increase their English proficiency because vocabulary was being recycled to mastery.

This Likely Won't Work

The focus of the reading lesson in this 2nd grade classroom was sequencing, and from the teacher's point of view it was a unifying concept. The two worksheets the students were completing, however, covered two very different topics—how to make an animal mask and how to make a compost pile, with completely different subject vocabulary. To top it off, the lesson was preceded by a read-aloud on how beavers make dams! Topic switching like this makes it difficult for ELLs to gain vocabulary mastery. For a lesson on sequencing, for example, it would be far better to have two different readings on the same topic. In this way, students can concentrate on learning the concept without learning so much new vocabulary. Trying to do both makes learning far more difficult than it needs to be for ELLs.

Digging Deeper–Authentic English

Adults, who often have limited time and clearly defined learning goals, study English for specific purposes. For example, they want to learn English for academic purposes, English for medical purposes, English for legal purposes, and so on. Sometimes the English taught in K–12 classrooms, however, is ENAP—English for no apparent purpose. Take a lesson from adults who are learning English for targeted goals and give your students many *authentic* reasons to use language. Your ELLs will learn academic English faster when they're using it for real purposes and not simply doing "make work" activities.

This Will Likely Work

Third grade students in a before-school program for ELLs submitted an application to an annual Kids to Parks Day free field trip contest. This contest stressed student involvement; students were encouraged to research the park they wanted to visit and write their own answers to the application questions. This is a good example of an authentic way to practice persuasive writing and meet Common Core State Standard ELA-Literacy.W.3.1—"Write opinion pieces on topics or texts, supporting a point of view with reasons" (Common Core State Standards Initiative 2019a). The students who worked on this Kids to Parks Day application, parts of which are shown in Figure 5.2, actually won a free field trip for themselves and the kindergarten classes they wanted to take with them. This was a great way to use English for a real purpose and get authentic feedback, too. The students knew their persuasive writing truly was persuasive because they won!

FIGURE 5.2 WRITING FOR AN AUTHENTIC PURPOSE

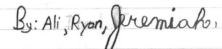

We are going to leave the park a better place by not making a mess or making animals eat plastic bottle by picking the trash up. We will make this place popular by telling Students to tell their friends and family members about it. We will follow the nature guide's instructions. The water in michigan is important for itself. After we go to Stony creek park we will learn how water important it is for michigan.

By: Ali, Ryan, Jeremiah,

This Likely Won't Work

A visitor's questions to an upper elementary ELL student and the student's responses:

Visitor: What are you doing now?
Student: We're making [a] crossword puzzle.
Visitor: What's the crossword puzzle about?

Student: Language arts.

Visitor: But what kind of words are you using for your crossword puzzle?

Student: Tier-one, tier-two, and tier-three words.

The student was using words from three lists: one with tier-one words (everyday language), one with tier-two words (academic vocabulary), and one with tier-three words (domain-specific words or words more typically found in content areas such as social studies or science). None of these lists had any unifying theme; even the tier-three words were from several different subject areas. It was clear to the student she needed to construct a crossword puzzle, but for spelling practice? Vocabulary practice? Social studies review? This looked like a case of ENAP. Another example of ENAP is shown in Figure 5.3. What was the teacher thinking? Well, in this case I know because I was the author who spent so much time creating this worksheet for students to spend so much time coloring. Looking back, I have to admit I was actually *trying* to make extra work for the students. Like many of my teaching colleagues who have come before and after me, I thought students *working* and students *learning* were the same thing. They're not. When students do work with no authentic meaning attached, it wastes everybody's time—teachers' and students' alike.

Making It Right in Your Classroom: Social Studies

Social studies is the content area in which ELLs will likely have the least background knowledge—or they'll have background knowledge, but it won't be the same as that of their classmates. A 5th grade newcomer once asked me to remind his social studies teacher that he hadn't studied Michigan history in El Salvador. His classmates had learned about Michigan history and geography as 4th graders, and he was confused by references to this previously studied material. He had attended school in his home country, so

FIGURE 5.3 EXAMPLE OF ENAP—ENGLISH FOR NO APPARENT PURPOSE

Name:_____

third   rat

try   aid   bat

hard   tray   day

hay   dairy   dry

1. Color all the words that rhyme with "hat" blue.
2. Color all the words that rhyme with "play" red.
3. Color the words that rhyme with "lie" orange.
4. Color the words that rhyme with "lard" purple.

he did have background knowledge; it just didn't match that of his classmates. I was impressed this student was perceptive enough to understand what was hampering his comprehension. I suppose he could have pointed this out to his general education teacher himself—he certainly had enough English skills to point it out to me—but I was happy to pass it on. ESL specialists often get information from their ELLs more easily than a general education teacher might because they work with these students in smaller groups. They may also speak their students' native languages. Keep this in mind and use your specialist's access to gain insights. My newcomer's reminder to his classroom teacher is a good one for all teachers. Newcomers have background knowledge, but it may not be the same as the majority of your students. For example, the newcomers sitting in your 11th grade American history class did not study American history in elementary school and middle school like most of their classmates did. Social studies is particularly vulnerable to this kind of background knowledge gap.

Another example in social studies comes from what happens whenever I use a map with my ELLs. No matter what location I point out—our suburb's location in comparison to Detroit or our state of Michigan in comparison to the rest of the United States—the students will invariably ask, "Where's Iraq?" That's because Iraq, their birthplace or that of their parents, is their frame of reference and the base of their background knowledge. What I should do first is start with what students know—point out Iraq on a world map so that they can see it in relation to new geographic locations being discussed. Learn from me and do it better—start with what your ELLs already know.

Digging Deeper–Visuals

Visuals are important for making content comprehensible for all ELLs but especially for newcomers, who are more likely to have basic English skills. Visuals are especially important to use in social studies, which is text driven. Language acquisition specialists are used to relying heavily on pictures by necessity; in contrast, general education teachers may be more accustomed to using words. "Barbara, how can I explain what an attic is?" a 1st grade teacher once asked when I walked into her classroom. The class was in the middle of a read-aloud, and questions had come up about where in the house the story was taking place. "Easy—just show them," I advised and used the teacher's computer to quickly find an image of an attic online to project on the whiteboard. The teacher was perceptive enough to understand that some words weren't getting through to her students. She just didn't realize her ELLs needed to *see* her explanation as well as *hear* it. In addition, showing the images led to more discussion about differences between an attic and other parts of a house, such as a basement.

I observed another example of the power of an image during a 4th grade discussion of a recipe. When the teacher asked the class if they knew what a spatula was, some students responded yes. Wisely ignoring this, she used a quick Internet search to find and project an image of a spatula on the whiteboard. From the audible gasps of understanding and the subsequent discussion, it was obvious many students had confused a spatula with a metal pancake turner. The students then pointed out the fine differences between the two utensils. Having students compare and contrast similar words builds *academic* language proficiency, something many ELLs don't have yet (Marzano, Pickering, & Pollock, 2012). In just a few seconds and with no preparation, this teacher helped her students understand the original passage and increased their vocabulary as well.

Visuals aren't just images; they can also include video clips, a book page projected on the document camera as it's being read aloud, or a projected copy of a handout or a text students are discussing. Make sure you have a dedicated projection space in your classroom free of written words or posted papers. Visuals are too important for students to have to get used to looking through distractions like printed words on the whiteboard or posters obscuring part of the view.

Figure 5.4 shows a visual used to prepare a class for a service-learning field trip to a local food bank warehouse. The teacher used this map not only to tell but also to *show* the students where they would be going on their field trip. The students could see exactly where they would be traveling, how far it would be, and how long it would take. This image also generated discussion about the merits of the different routes shown—a chance for students to practice more complex thinking. In addition, the teacher used a laser pointer to focus students' attention as she discussed specific details on the map. ("See, here is I-696, the interstate. Do you see the red rectangles? What do you think they mean?")

FIGURE 5.4   USING VISUALS TO MAKE CONTENT COMPREHENSIBLE

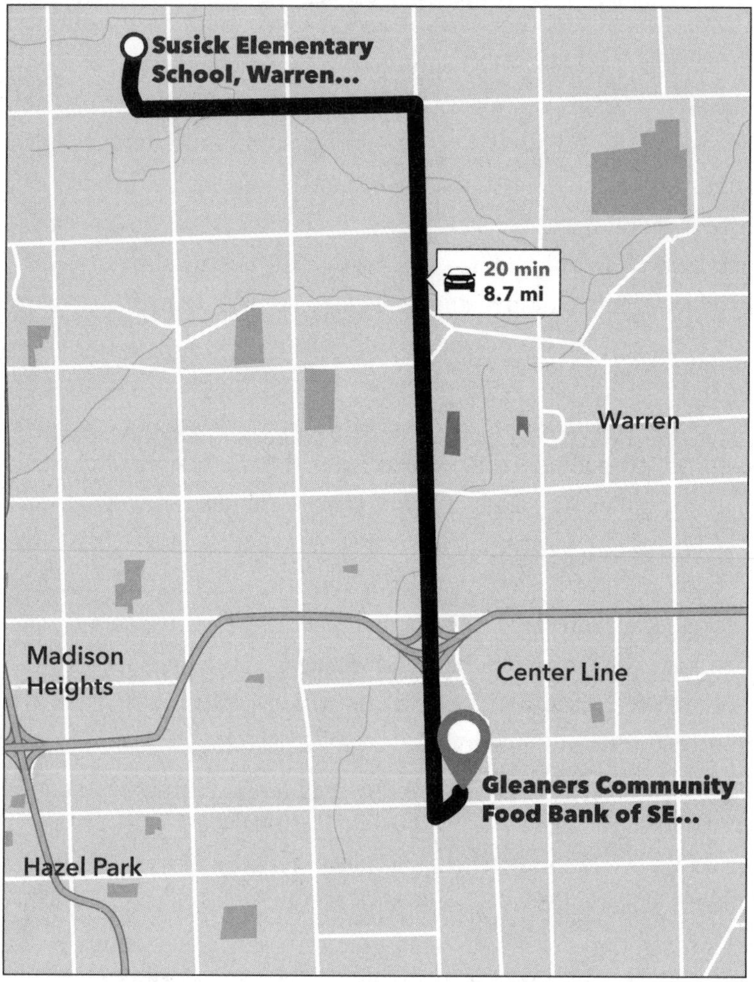

The printed page can also be a helpful visual for aural input—for example, when a teacher is reading a chapter book aloud to the class. I've known teachers who were reluctant to allow ELLs to read along in copies of a chapter book being read aloud to the class. "I want the students to really concentrate on listening," they said. The reasoning against this support is akin to telling someone with bad eyesight that they can train their eyes to see better if they just "really concentrate" when they read. In the same way eyeglasses level the playing field so that people who need them can see as well as those who don't need the assistance, reading along in the book while the teacher is reading aloud to the class levels the playing field for ELLs because it *helps* their comprehension. It's even better if the teacher gives this opportunity to the entire class by using a document camera to project the pages of a book. Students can read along silently and view any illustrations as the teacher reads. The read-aloud then becomes a more shared experience.

Making It Right in Your Classroom: Science

A general education teacher, who was genuinely surprised by an activity I had done with my 4th and 5th grade newcomers, once said to me, "They can do that?" I've long since forgotten what the activity was, mainly because "that" referred to activities the newcomers did every day. The unusual part was that I'd mentioned it to my colleague. She was surprised my students could "do that," but she shouldn't have been. Science is a content area in which newcomer ELLs easily "can do that" if they have proper supports. Unlike with social studies, lack of cultural background knowledge won't pose as much of a problem in science. Understanding the three states of matter, for example, or learning about plant life, involves much more universal concepts than American government or Texas history. Elementary teachers can use this to their advantage by using nonfiction science texts in the language arts block. The Common Core State Standards' increased emphasis on nonfiction helps ELLs, since such reading selections are not as culture bound as fiction. They also do valuable double duty, serving as a reading text and building science content knowledge at the same time. ELLs may not have as much experience with lab experiments and other hands-on science activities, but they are also more likely to be successful with them. Just make sure students get practice in all four domains—listening, speaking, reading, and writing—when doing these activities.

The following example involves a service-learning project, but it's also relevant to the kinds of hands-on activities students do in science. It illustrates the importance of giving students practice in talking about what they are doing:

> A group of 5th grade students made fleece blankets for a local children's hospital as a service-learning project. They viewed a video about how to make the blankets, listened to follow-up explanations from their teacher, and made the blankets in small groups. One might assume this would have helped the students remember the relevant academic vocabulary, but when the students—even non-ELL students—were asked later to explain photos from the activity, they didn't have the vocabulary to talk clearly about what they had done. They had used items like fleece and masking tape, and they had done things like cutting the fleece into strips and tying it into knots, but they hadn't spent enough time talking and writing about what they had done to make the vocabulary stick. As a result, they couldn't precisely describe what was happening in the photos.

The activity could have been improved by having the students read the instructions for making a fleece blanket before viewing the how-to video and noting similarities and differences between the two different methods. That would have added practice in reading, an additional language domain. Simply noting key vocabulary for the activity and writing the words on the board also would have helped students use the correct academic vocabulary during the activity. These supports might have helped students say, "Those strips are too wide" rather than "That's too big" or "Can I have some more fleece?" rather than "Can I have some of that stuff there?" Students could have gotten writing practice after the activity by using the correct vocabulary to describe the steps they had completed. Practice in all four domains would have helped the students retain the academic vocabulary. Similar hands-on activities are often done during science classes. They're great for ELLs, but they can be improved by incorporating practice in all four language domains. Before they start the activity, you can have students do something as simple as explain to a partner what they are going to do. After the activity, students can write about what they did using key vocabulary.

A LITTLE EXTRA . . .

- Mary Pipher, a psychologist in Lincoln, Nebraska, is well-known for *Reviving Ophelia,* her book about helping young girls enter adulthood, but her more obscure book, *The Middle of Everywhere: Helping Refugees Enter the American Community,* is a must-read for anyone wanting to learn more about refugees and other newcomers to the United States. She points out that immigrants will learn soon enough on their own about the parts of American culture we're not so proud of–the junk food, the bad movies, and the rampant consumerism. Instead, Pipher says, we have an obligation to show newcomers the many good things our country offers–our parks, our libraries, our free festivals, our museums, and the like. Years after reading her book, I still took to heart her advice when planning field trips and activities for students, trying to introduce them to good things they might not discover on their own.

- Ask your school's attendance clerk for the birthplaces of your students. Elementary students, especially, may have been schooled entirely in the United States, but being born outside of the United States indicates a relatively new immigrant family. Time in the United States isn't an accurate proxy for any family member's English language ability, but it will give you an idea of a family's familiarity with the United States. Your attendance clerk can also tell you when schooling began in the United States for your older ELLs. Your "newcomer" may turn out to be new to you but not so new to the United States.

- Visit www.louisianabelieves.com/resources/library/teacher-support-toolbox-library for a good source of text sets to help you teach thematically. Created by the Louisiana Department of Education, this website has thematic resources for all subjects and all grade levels.

Conclusion

This chapter and Chapter 4 have shown you how to reach new-comers, the students we usually think of first when we hear the term "English language learner." You've learned their needs are great, but in some ways that's a plus because it's obvious to their teachers. The next chapter will introduce you to a very different kind of ELL whose needs are not so obvious. These students need special teaching just as much as newcomers, but you may not even be aware they are in your classroom. Read on to find out how they are managing to hide in plain sight.

ELLs Hiding in Plain Sight

MISCONCEPTION: "OH, THE NEW STUDENT WILL BE FINE. HE SPEAKS ENGLISH."

This chapter shines a light on the overlooked ELL. It discusses the process of developing academic English language and how it can take years to develop full *academic* proficiency. You'll learn why it's important not to assume proficiency based on everyday spoken English and get tips on how to ensure your ELLs get practice using and thus developing their academic English.

The Problem with This Misconception

The title of this chapter is not quite accurate. Students experiencing academic difficulties are painfully obvious to their teachers; they are not hiding in plain sight at all. What is not so obvious is that these students may still be ELLs. Widely recognized research in the field has shown that ELLs can take five to seven years to gain academic English proficiency (Collier, 1987; Hakuta, Butler, & Witt, 2000; Thomas & Collier, 1997). The National Academy of Sciences, Engineering, and Medicine (2017) reviewed a large sample of key studies on time to reclassification and found "notwithstanding variation in the estimates of time to proficiency across studies, they all indicate that ELs require several grades or years to be rated proficient—five to seven years is frequently reported" (p. 225). For most purposes, proficiency is defined as the time it takes for an ELL to be reclassified as a former ELL. For secondary students with limited or interrupted schooling, called SIFE (students with interrupted formal education), acquiring academic proficiency presents a particularly difficult challenge. The reasons for limited or interrupted schooling are as diverse as the students themselves. Students may have been living in exile as refugees in countries where they were not able to attend public school, or the school they were able to attend did not offer as much programming as that of a U.S. public school. Students may also move back and forth between the United States and their home countries, missing significant periods of school time in the process. Research done on a national-level sample of 10th graders found that SIFE students accounted for 11 percent of foreign-born youth, higher than previously thought (Potochnick, 2018). The study also found that students with interrupted schooling were at least as engaged with school as their peers. Regardless of the causes of their limited schooling, this indicates SIFE students are likely motivated to begin, complete, or at least get some of their education in your school.

While ELLs are progressing toward proficiency, they can often "pass" as proficient. That's because teachers, like the one quoted at the beginning of this chapter, often make assumptions about the ability level of ELLs based on their oral fluency in social English. The teacher quoted said the new student "speaks English," but this viewpoint doesn't acknowledge that full English proficiency includes four domains—listening, speaking, reading, and writing. Speaking is only one of these domains. Even the U.S. Census Bureau helps to further this misconception. Its survey questions ask families about the language spoken at home and to assess how well family members *speak English*, which represents just

25 percent of total English proficiency. I don't think the Census Bureau is asking about speaking ability because it's interested in only this domain. Instead, I have a hunch it's making the mistake a lot of people do and extrapolating speaking ability to overall English proficiency. They are not the same thing. Listen closely to your ELL student who is speaking what seems to be fluent English with perfect pronunciation. You may start to notice the student is simply saying one of the following:

- Standard phrases: "May I have a hall pass?" "I forgot my book."
- Social or "recess" English: "That's awesome!" "I don't get it."
- Responses to questions requiring only one-word or short answers: "Yes," "No," "The Gulf of Mexico."

The "fluent" English a student is speaking actually comes from a limited social vocabulary of high-frequency words. Cummins (1999), a leader in second-language acquisition, has been reminding us for years about the distinction between social and academic English. He calls the former "BICS"—basic interpersonal communicative skills—which is the social English that ELLs can learn in one or two years. It is highly contextualized, and examples include asking to go to the bathroom, talking about the weekend with friends, and discussing the food options in the school cafeteria. CALP—cognitive academic language proficiency—by contrast, is the "school English" that takes much longer for ELLs to master. It is decontextualized and uses vocabulary students typically encounter only in school and in reading. The importance of CALP increases from 3rd grade on, when texts begin using more academic vocabulary not encountered in everyday life. Examples of CALP include summarizing a paragraph in a science textbook, writing in a math journal about how a word problem was solved, and verifying a news source's reliability. BICS is like the appetizer in a meal while CALP is like the entrée. Students can get by using the high-frequency social vocabulary of BICS appetizers, but to get their school hunger fully satisfied, they're going to need the entrée—CALP.

Most monolingual Americans never get past BICS in their high school foreign language courses. I know I never did, even though I lived for two years in Japan as an English teacher. I was functionally illiterate, but my spoken Japanese was good enough to order food in a restaurant, watch cooking shows on Japanese TV, and discuss the weather with my Japanese neighbor. At the same time, I quickly became lost listening to political talk shows, couldn't make sense of the front page of a Japanese newspaper, and could understand a TV news story only if it had pictures. In short, I had BICS—the language that was social, face-to-face, and highly contextualized—but not CALP.

I have seen the limits of BICS firsthand with a bilingual colleague. "I don't know how to say 'paragraph' in Arabic," my team-teaching partner whispered apologetically to me once as the two of us were trying to explain a writing assignment to our Arabic-speaking newcomers. I certainly understood; after all, I couldn't say *anything* in Arabic. Born in the United States and educated in English, my colleague was a heritage speaker of Arabic because she had grown up in an Arabic-speaking family. She realized, however, after she became a teacher and started to use her bilingual skills in a school setting, that her Arabic consisted mostly of BICS, not CALP.

Setting This Misconception Straight

So, what can you do to correct the misconception that oral English proficiency equals total English proficiency? How will this benefit your students?

Educate Yourself

Educate yourself and everyone else, including your students, about the time it takes to reach proficiency. My friend, a community college ESL instructor, once told one of her developmental ESL students about the research showing the length of time it takes to reach full academic English proficiency. The student, who had graduated from an American high school, seemed relieved and said, "Oh, I just thought I was stupid." She was ashamed to be in community college ESL courses after living for several years in the United States, but she shouldn't have been. Her experience simply reflected what research tells us about how long it takes students to learn academic English. The feel-good story on the local TV news, for example, about the student who wins the state spelling bee after living just a few years in the United States is wonderful to hear, but outliers like this set up unrealistic expectations for all ELLs. Grade-level academic English isn't something one just "picks up." Awareness of the research on normal language acquisition can set everyone free.

Focus on Progress Toward Proficiency

Yes, it takes time to reach proficiency, but that doesn't mean we shouldn't hold our ELLs accountable. Instead, we should focus on *progress* toward proficiency. Media reports bemoaning the low passing rates of ELLs on standardized assessments are looking at the data incorrectly. They are holding ELLs and their teachers accountable for the wrong things. *English language learner* is not a static label like ethnicity. The ELL ranks are changing constantly—students leave as they reach proficiency and are reclassified, and students enter as they begin schooling in the United States. An English language learner is, by definition, still not fully proficient in English. It should come as no particular surprise, then, that ELLs often do not do well on standardized assessments. Rather than indicating a failing on the part of ELLs and their teachers, this simply proves that English language proficiency is necessary to achieve proficiency on other standardized assessments. That's a good thing—it tells us all these assessments are closely aligned.

A better accountability measure would be to determine *how long* the ELLs who are not passing the standardized tests have been ELLs and what has been their *rate of growth* toward proficiency.

English language acquisition is a developmental process. We should be looking at longitudinal data showing satisfactory growth instead of wondering why ELLs are not passing standardized assessments at rates comparable to those of non-ELLs. I found this out for myself when I assembled data on students at my school one year. Once ELLs reached proficiency, their passing percentage rates on the state math and language arts tests were just as good or even better than never ELLs. An analysis of scores on the National Assessment of Educational Progress also found no statistically significant difference between the performance of former ELLs and never ELLs on both the math and reading assessments (Wilde, 2010). Once students reach English proficiency, achievement on other standardized tests takes care of itself.

Remember Where the ELL Started

Teachers need to pay attention to where an ELL student started; that's key when looking at growth. Progress is faster at lower proficiency levels and lower grade levels. A 1st grade basic ELL will make faster progress than a 10th grade advanced ELL (WIDA Consortium, 2018). This is why it is important to compare the progress of an ELL student to other students at similar starting grades and proficiency levels.

Finally, knowing whether your students are ELLs is key. Menken, Funk, and Kleyn (2011) have done extensive research on long-term ELLs and found that simply increasing awareness about this population seems to have a positive impact on educational outcomes for these students. If you are a secondary teacher, do your students (or you) even realize they are still ELLs and have not been reclassified? I've seen cases where high school teachers and counselors knew, for example, that a student was from a Spanish-speaking family but had no idea whether the student was an ELL. The students themselves didn't know for sure, either. It's true that ELL status is just one of many factors that can affect a student's academic achievement. Still, it's a significant part of a student's history and should not be overlooked or, worse, ignored. Secondary teachers should especially note that ELL status is also a key indicator of the possibility of dropping out of high school. According to the National Center for Education Statistics (2013–14), the high school graduation rate for ELLs is 20 percentage points lower than the graduation rate for the general population. Simply knowing the number and percentage of ELLs in your school will help you to help them.

Digging Deeper–Oral Language

Clearly, not yet mastering academic "school English" (CALP) is a huge barrier to success for ELLs. Short and Fitzsimmons (2007) even refer to it as an "academic literacy crisis." Since ELLs typically develop strong oral language for social purposes (BICS) in just a year or two, you can build on this strength by increasing your students' opportunities to use oral English for academic purposes (CALP). Talking about what they are studying is the best way for students to make academic vocabulary stick, and it works at all grade levels. One of the key conclusions of a National Literacy Panel review of research on how language-minority children learn to read and write was that oral proficiency in English is a critical factor often overlooked in instruction (August, 2006). Teaching students to read in their first, or native, language assumes a strong oral foundation in the first language. With ELLs, that may not be the case because English is not their first language. In addition, a consensus study report by the National Academies of Sciences, Engineering, and Medicine (2017) pointed out that oral language proficiency is important for ELLs learning content. Teachers, however, need to mindfully create opportunities for oral language practice and not leave it to chance. It is possible, and unfortunately it happens far too often, for a student to get through an entire school day without uttering a single word of academic English. Too often, students are learning how to spell words they can't pronounce, writing answers to social studies comprehension questions using terms they can't talk about, and conducting science experiments they can't describe. Teachers will confidently claim, "We talked about it," when in fact, *they* talked about it, not the students. It is true that whole group discussion can be oral language practice—but only for the small percentage of students who contribute. Pair or small-group activities are a better way to efficiently get many students using academic English with each other.

Consider this exchange between two teachers about a morning meeting:

> **Teacher #1:** Why don't you have the students talk about their weekend in pairs before coming to the carpet and discussing as a group? That way ELLs could prepare.

> **Teacher #2:** Yeah, I know. But we're just doing it for a few minutes on Monday. We don't have time.

This exchange points out a misconception many teachers have about oral language activities—they're just something students do "for a few minutes on Mondays" because they're really not that important. You've already learned that research shows this isn't the case. This conversation also points out what teachers see as a disadvantage of oral language activities, even if they do believe in their value—they take too much time. However, if students do speaking activities often and procedures are in place, they don't need to take up much time. One of my teaching colleagues who often uses "turn and talk" effectively points out that such activities can *save* time. For example, during a 1st grade social studies lesson this teacher was beginning on communities, instead of listening to five different children describe their homes to the whole group, *all* the students in her class got a chance to describe their homes through pair work. After a short time with one partner, students moved to another partner and then another partner. They had a chance to hear other students' stories and get practice telling their story better and better each time they rotated to a new partner—in total, three different times. The teacher circulated among the pairs, providing individual feedback and support and noting points to make in the whole group wrap-up discussion after the activity. Students got more individual teacher attention and three times the language practice in the same amount of time!

Having students give presentations about what they are studying is a common way to have students practice speaking, especially at the secondary level. This strategy suffers, however, from the same disadvantage as whole group discussion—it's a relatively inefficient way to give all students speaking practice because only one student at a time is talking. Students need opportunities to talk about what they are presenting *throughout* the process of preparing a presentation. Speaking should be not only the end product but also part of the process. In fact, there's some evidence this would be useful for and welcomed by all students, not just ELLs. An article in *The Atlantic* magazine reported on a Twitter campaign waged by middle and high school students to get in-class presentations abolished on the grounds that they place too much stress on students who have public-speaking anxiety (Lorenz, 2018). In-class presentations and other kinds of public speaking assignments would cause far less anxiety if students had opportunities to practice what they were going to say with a partner or in a small group before speaking to the whole class.

This Will Likely Work

Here's an example of an oral language activity that works at all grade levels and in all subjects. Students who are more proficient readers can use index cards with a key vocabulary word written on each card, while less capable readers can use picture word cards. Give 5–10 cards to each student and put them in pairs. Students then explain each word to their partners without saying it, trying to get them to guess the words. For example:

Student A: It's a roundish red fruit.
Student B: Apple?
Student A: No, it's small and has seeds on the outside.
Student B: Strawberry?
Student A: Right!

And so on. When a pair of students has guessed all their words or when a set amount of time (say, three minutes) has elapsed, a student from each pair rotates to another partner for more practice. Customize the card decks by taking words out of the decks as students master them and adding other words as new content is studied. I've used this activity with 2nd graders up to graduate students. As I circulate and listen to the student pairs during this activity, I've never failed to gain insights into students' understanding (and misunderstanding!) of key vocabulary. This gives me valuable information to share with everyone during the activity wrap-up. If activities like this are done daily, students have multiple opportunities for exposure to the new words, the best way to permanently acquire academic vocabulary.

Another way to ensure that academic vocabulary "sticks" is to provide opportunities for students to practice using the language not only in speaking but also in the other three domains. Providing multiple opportunities to engage with the content will help students acquire the academic vocabulary. It also saves time in that students don't have to relearn the same concepts every year because they had only a surface understanding of them in the first place. Teachers who "don't have time" to ensure that students speak, listen, read, and write about a topic confuse covering it with students *learning* about it. Less is more.

I contributed the following excerpt to *Hands On English*, a newsletter for ESL teachers (Gottschalk, 1994). The advice is old but still online, and the point it makes about ensuring students have the opportunity to use all four language domains when doing any kind of activity still holds true:

> This suggestion is both a time-saver and good pedagogy. Barbara Gottschalk has seen many teachers rush from worksheet to worksheet and textbook to textbook, wearing out themselves and the copy machine in the process! It is sounder teaching practice to fully expand on each item you present.
>
> Here is a checklist of questions that Barbara suggests we ask, for example, about a story the students have read: Have they talked about it? Have they talked to each other about it? Have they written about it? Have they written about what someone else said about it? Have they read what other students have written about it? Have they done a dictation about it for listening practice? The repetition such activities provides is very important for language learning.

Ironically, I wrote this to help busy teachers of adult ELLs save time, but these suggestions also help K–12 students. Teachers sometimes say they don't want to bore their more able students by having them do a variety of activities on a topic, but they fail to realize this builds mastery. Before you move on to the next topic, make sure your students have engaged with the content using all four language domains. This will help your long-term ELLs to develop academic English.

This, Too, Will Likely Work

Don't think you have time for students to practice all four domains? Combine them! For example, end your lesson with a particularly thoughtful question. Give your students several minutes to compose a written answer, then have them share with partners before discussing answers as a whole group. This gives everyone writing and speaking practice. It also gives students a chance to rehearse their answers before participating in a whole group discussion, which is especially helpful to ELLs who might otherwise hesitate to contribute.

Digging Deeper–Questions

"Ms. Gottschalk, don't you get it?" The little 1st grade ELL asking me this question seemed genuinely concerned I was losing my mind. He was perplexed because I kept asking him and his classmates questions whose answers I already knew. In other words, I was asking *display questions* like these: "This girl is sitting. What is she doing?" "This girl is standing. What is she doing?" "Is the balloon on the elephant?" "Is the balloon behind the elephant?" and so on. In the middle of the year, I had changed my pull-out sessions with lower-level ELLs to begin using my district's newly adopted direct instruction intervention program. My student's question to me pointed out the scripted curriculum's biggest drawback—its lack of authentic communication. It was apparent to this young ELL because I had spent much of our time together in the first part of the school year asking *referential questions*—questions whose answers I didn't already know, such as these:

- Which of these books I've read aloud did you like the best? Why?
- What was your favorite illustration in this picture book we've just read together? Can you describe it clearly enough so I can find it in the book?
- I missed meeting with you yesterday because of your field trip. Which part of the field trip did you like best and why?

There's a place for display questions in your teaching toolkit, but asking display questions of individual students during a group discussion is an inefficient way to assess knowledge. Having students answer these questions in pairs or small groups provides more speaking practice, but if students have mastered the content, they're still asking each other questions whose answers everybody already knows. That's not real communication. In contrast, notice in Figure 6.1 how referential questions elicit the same kind of information as display questions but also require students to draw on their own opinions or experience. Even if your students aren't

FIGURE 6.1 DISPLAY QUESTIONS VERSUS REFERENTIAL QUESTIONS

Display	Referential
"What was the main point of this video clip?"	"What is one thing you remember most from the video clip? Why?"
"What does frustrate mean?"	"What is something that frustrates you? Why?"
"What is the past tense of *catch*?"	"Tell me about the last time you *caught* a cold."
"What is one trait of the main character in this story?"	"What is one trait you have in common with the main character in this story?"

convinced, speaking practice will help them learn better and faster. The right kind of practice at least encourages them to try. Answering referential questions motivates students because it allows them to apply their knowledge and also share information about themselves. That's why one easy way to promote speaking with ELLs is for teachers and students alike to ask each other more referential questions.

A LITTLE EXTRA . . .

Stealing Buddha's Dinner by Bich Minh Nguyen is a memoir of a Vietnamese girl growing up in Grand Rapids, Michigan. It was chosen as a Great Michigan Reads book for 2009–2010, but it's far more than a Michigan story. The author comes from a multicultural blended family, and her story of how American food makes her American is an interesting take on the immigrant experience.

Conclusion

Even though an ELL's spoken English may appear fluent ("Oh, the new student will be fine. He speaks English."), it still doesn't mean the ELL is fully English proficient, especially when academic English proficiency is considered. ELLs need opportunities to use the academic English they're learning. In fact, using English in all four domains will help cement understanding. The next chapter will help you acknowledge what your ELLs already know and then build on it.

Acknowledging Knowledge

MISCONCEPTION: "MS. G., THE NEW GIRL, SHE DON'T KNOW *ANYTHING!*"

Why is background knowledge so important for ELLs? Like an interest-bearing savings account, background knowledge builds greater value when it starts early. It's the gift that keeps on giving. This chapter will help you immediately begin building background knowledge for your ELLs. You'll get tips on how to make your instruction more comprehensible and relevant by using what your students already know.

The Problem with This Misconception

It may appear to a lot of people—like the newcomer quoted at the beginning of this chapter, commenting with concern and shock about a new classmate—that students who don't know English don't know much of anything else. *That's not the case!* ELLs aren't empty vessels; every student comes to us with a wealth of knowledge and experiences. The challenge is that often our students' knowledge and experiences aren't as helpful to them in a different context. Even students born in the United States have experiences that give them different perspectives. I once listened during a paired speaking activity as a 3rd grade ELL tried to give clues so that his partner could identify the word *earthquake*. The boy's first clue sentence was, "They had this in Iraq last November." I had no idea what he meant, but the other student immediately said, "Earthquake." These ELLs were born in the United States, but they both knew about this recent event in Iraq, their parents' home country. I, by contrast, never would have guessed the correct word from that one clue because I didn't have the appropriate background knowledge. Like these ELLs, other students have background knowledge too. Our job is to find out what it is and to link that knowledge to all the new experiences students get in school.

All students, not just ELLs, come to us with different background knowledge that teachers would be wise to acknowledge. A good example is the Mindset List, created in 1998 by three professors at Beloit College. Every year since then, the Mindset List has reminded college teachers how different their worldview is from that of their entering first-year students. An example from the Mindset List for the class of 2022 is that these students, unlike their teachers, have never used a spit bowl in a dentist's office and have always been able to use Wikipedia (McBride, Nief, & Westerberg, 2018). "Students come to college with particular assumptions based on the horizons of their lived experience," says Tom McBride, one of the original authors of the list. Just like college students, our ELLs also come to us with "particular assumptions based on the horizons of their lived experience."

Beyond simply acknowledging your students' different background knowledge, make sure you also value it. Some teachers at my school used to disapprove of an ELL family visiting the home country every summer. The teachers thought the children's summer was "wasted" because they weren't speaking English. I thought summer vacations in the home country sounded like a great idea. Some children returned to school in the fall with happy stories of living on a farm with their extended relatives. This established familial connections and provided an enriching experience for these city children. It also strengthened the children's home language. What's not to like about that? Nothing, really, but the children's teachers failed to see the positive part of it. Acknowledge and appreciate your ELLs' different experiences.

Setting This Misconception Straight

So, if it's a misconception that ELLs don't know anything, then find out what they *do* know so that you can use this information. It has been my experience, unfortunately, that new students can show up at a school before the school receives any information from the student's prior records. If this happens, don't forget to follow up later. Parent–teacher conferences are a good time to find out more about a student's history. Asking about previous schooling in the home country or at other schools the student has attended in the United States allows parents to share information as the experts. Many teachers spend too much time in conferences talking and not enough time listening to parents. Asking parents, "Do you have any questions about what I've explained?" represents the kind of closed question that's not helpful. Even though it takes time, asking open-ended questions like these will help you fill in the blanks about a student's history:

- What is the biggest difference between Yousif's school before and his school now?
- Is Yousif happy to come to school? Why or why not?
- Is there a particular reason Yousif is transferring to this school (for example, is the student switching schools but not moving)?

You can probably think of even better open-ended questions about your own students. Just don't feel guilty about taking time to ask parents these questions during conferences.

Making It Right in Your Classroom

Ironically, we teachers are the ones most likely to assume background knowledge simply because of our biographies. Studies of teacher mobility find that teachers aren't very mobile. Most teachers start teaching close to home and stay there. For example, Goldring, Taie, and Riddles (2014) did a teacher mobility study for the National Center for Education Statistics and found that 84 percent of America's teachers in 2012–2013 were teaching in the same school they had taught in the year before. In a survey for the National Center for Education Information, Feistritzer (2011) found that 57 percent of traditionally trained teachers were teaching within 150 miles of where they were born. There's nothing wrong with staying close to where you started, but it makes most teachers' lived experience different from that of their more transient ELLs.

Sometimes we fail to remember this. I learned for myself when I moved to a new state and was one of just a few teachers on my school's staff from outside the immediate area, let alone a different state. My well-meaning principal kept saying in memos and announcements that we'd be doing something "like last year." It made sense to everybody but me because *I hadn't been there last year.* Compare this to how another, more helpful principal always began explanations in staff meetings with "I realize some of you are already familiar with this, but for the new people on staff . . . ." Invariably people who were "already familiar with this" ended up asking just as many questions as the new people. The teachers with previous knowledge had additional ways to view the already familiar information (prior knowledge) and that generated more sophisticated questions. It can work the same way in your classroom. Statistically, your ELLs are more likely to be newer to your school, city, state, or country than you are. Don't forget that. And don't forget that the review, revisiting, and recycling you do to help them build relevant background can also benefit other students who are "already familiar with this," in the same way it did for the teachers in my school's staff meetings.

Like my helpful principal, be careful to "frame" your lessons by recapping what went before when starting a lesson and reviewing what has happened when finishing a lesson. For example, before beginning the next chapter in a read-aloud, have students in pairs retell what happened in the previous chapter. This helps students who were absent or those who may not have understood the first time around. Remember, it may seem like pointless repetition to you, but it's valuable recycling for ELLs. ELLs are always playing catch up—can you imagine how great it must feel to finally get the time and opportunities to understand? For example, every year in the month before Valentine's Day, my 2nd grade teacher colleagues had their students write letters to each day's special student, describing what was special about that student and what they liked about him. Teachers used the same sentence stems and added words to a word bank as needed during the month. Teachers told me they got bored with it before students had finished writing about even half of their classmates, but the students didn't. Practice didn't make perfect, but it certainly made the students' writing richer and more developed by the end of the activity.

Digging Deeper–Building Background Knowledge

So, your ELLs have background knowledge, but you realize it's not going to fit what you're studying. In that case, help your students build it. Background knowledge—the information and experiences students already have about a topic—helps students make links to new information. It also is a key reason students can comprehend a text written at a higher reading level than what they might normally be able to read. A panel of experts convened in 2018 to discuss reasons for the relatively flat reading scores of

U.S. students since 1998 on the National Assessment of Educational Progress or NAEP (National Assessment Governing Board, 2018). These experts concluded that building general background knowledge has been given short shrift, crowded out by a narrowing of the curriculum and too much instructional time spent on teaching reading strategies. One of these experts pointed out that many studies show good readers use reading strategies, but far few studies show reading strategies *cause* good reading comprehension (Willingham, 2006–2007). Reading strategy instruction does work, but to make good readers, teachers should spend far more time building students' knowledge and vocabulary (Willingham & Lovette, 2014). Noted educator E. D. Hirsch would agree. In his 2006 book *The Knowledge Deficit*, he argued that schools do a good job of teaching the mechanics of reading but blamed insufficient background knowledge for the far-too-common slump in reading comprehension beginning in the upper elementary grades.

I saw for myself how this played out in data intervention meetings for at-risk students, many of them ELLs. Lower elementary classroom teachers often noted students needed to master phonemic awareness skills for their reading to improve. Then in the middle grades, after their students had mastered the mechanics of reading, teachers would say comprehension was a problem. In too many reading lessons, the point wasn't to learn about the content (pelicans, Ruby Bridges, or how bees make honey). Rather, the point was to teach a reading strategy like inferring, sequencing, or finding the main idea. After I realized this, I started to understand why teachers would tell me they didn't have time to show video clips or use another text to develop the topic of a reading lesson. The strategy, not the content, was the focus of the lesson. Research by Recht and Leslie (1988), however, says that's the wrong approach. In their study, they preassessed 7th and 8th grade students for reading comprehension ability and for prior knowledge of baseball. They had students read a passage describing a half inning of a baseball game and then perform various recall, retell, summarizing, and sorting activities. They found students with high knowledge of baseball and low reading ability performed just as well as students with low knowledge of baseball and high reading ability. In other words, prior knowledge made up for poor reading skills. The authors of this study concluded that reading strategy instruction isn't enough; attention to building students' knowledge base through prereading activities is also important. For ELLs, it's not just important; it's essential.

ELLs are similar to other at-risk students if they simply need more relevant knowledge and experience. For example, all students in a rural community may need to learn about what a subway is before reading *The Cricket in Times Square*, a children's novel set in a New York subway station. At the same time, ELLs may especially need background building for topics that assume specific culture-based prior knowledge. A student from China will need to understand what a tamale is and how it's made before comprehending and enjoying *Too Many Tamales*, a story about a girl who loses her ring while making tamales for the holidays. A Spanish-speaking student may be familiar with this custom. This is why it's a good idea, if possible, to use culturally relevant topics that students might already understand and know something about. Here's another example: Students at my school once saw a performance of an opera based on *How Nanita Learned to Make Flan*, a picture book that incorporates many elements of Mexican culture. Everyone enjoyed the opera, but the Spanish-speaking students in particular knew all about what was going on in the story—the flan, the first Communion, the song lyrics in Spanish, and the like. Once again, this reminded me of the importance of prior knowledge—and, in its absence, building some for everybody. ELLs bring many experiences and much knowledge to the classroom. The difficulty arises when that experience and knowledge don't match what's being studied. A wise teacher will realize this and ensure all students have the necessary background before studying a topic. Even difficult concepts can be covered and higher-order thinking skills employed if students have sufficient background knowledge.

This Will Likely Work

A school's media specialist built background knowledge for the entire student body before a touring opera company's performance of a children's opera, *The Araboolies of Liberty Street*. She did this by reading aloud the picture book on which the opera was based to all the media classes in the week before the assembly. Before the performance, the singers asked the audience, "How many of you know the story *The Araboolies of Liberty Street*?" The performers were pleased but seemed surprised when all the students raised their hands.

This Likely Won't Work

The same opera company had performed *The Araboolies of Liberty Street* at another school the previous year. The principal there sheepishly admitted background building had been limited to the six students chosen to play the student roles in the opera. She had called the students down to her office and read the story aloud to them; other students in the school didn't read the book and saw the opera "cold." Imagine how much richer the experience was at the school where all students learned about the story of the opera before seeing the performance.

Don't save background building just for special activities. The following examples of daily writing prompts for lower elementary students show why background building is imperative for even the most ordinary of classroom activities:

- A toothpick can be . . .
- Her baton went up so high . . .
- Oscar Octopus could not find his . . .

Nothing is inherently wrong with any of these prompts, but students were expected to individually choose a prompt and write about it at the beginning of the school day, while the teacher was taking attendance, completing lunch count, and so on. This "bell work" might be difficult for ELLs because students had to respond in writing without any kind of preparation. Students chose the prompts they wanted to use from a monthly calendar, so they weren't stuck with a particularly incomprehensible topic for the day. Still, students would have produced much better writing if the teacher had brainstormed a word bank of essential vocabulary with the students and given them an opportunity to discuss the day's prompt before writing. "Cold" activities aren't effective for any student, but they especially put ELLs at a disadvantage. What starts out as an attempt to personalize the activity—everybody can write about the topic they find most interesting—ends up being unnecessarily difficult. When students say, "I don't know what to write about," what they really mean is, "I need help building background knowledge."

Digging Deeper–Creating Shared Experiences

Experiences, but especially those ELLs share with their classmates, help level the playing field because everyone starts with a similar background knowledge base. A shared experience can be as elaborate as a field trip, or something as simple as a video clip, a book read aloud, or a class demonstration—many things can suffice, as long as students experience them together. Once that is accomplished, teachers can use these shared experiences as springboards to other listening, speaking, reading, and writing activities.

A good example of a shared experience, in both the literal and the figurative sense, is a project at my school that involved students visiting a nearby senior living facility to interview residents about their lives. The first visit was for initial interviews of individual residents by groups of three or four students; on the second visit, students shared their rough drafts with the residents and asked follow-up questions. Back at school, the students worked together to write a life story about each of the residents they had interviewed. Each student was responsible for a particular section of the life story, but they all had input because they'd participated in the interviews. On the third and final visit, students shared the completed life stories with the residents. Listening and speaking served as a springboard for student reading and writing, giving students practice in all four domains. In addition, students were creating a *shared* experience with their senior friends and with each other as they worked on the life stories.

A colleague of mine once remarked to me about her 1st graders' papers about their field trip to the zoo, "I was kind of surprised at how well they wrote." I wasn't. Her students had been well prepared before their field trip to the zoo, the class had written a model story about it together when they returned, and they'd also had a chance to talk with each other about what they liked best about the field trip before writing about it. After all of that background building, her students could confidently write about their zoo field trip on their own. In contrast, another colleague told me she was disappointed with her students' responses to this writing prompt: "If you could invent an ice cream flavor, what would it be?" She realized belatedly that many students weren't familiar with the names of ice cream flavors. Most students have experience eating ice cream, but they might not know their favorite flavor is "Double Dunker" or "Guatemalan Ripple." A student would need to know various flavors of ice cream and their names before being able to write cleverly about an imaginary ice cream flavor. By contrast, the 1st grade students were able to easily write well about their field trip to the zoo. They got a chance to personalize the assignment by writing about their favorite part of the zoo, but they still had the support of a shared experience—the field trip and its accompanying activities. Students who were writing about an imaginary ice cream flavor had to think of everything on their own. An assignment the teacher mistakenly assumed would be easy for her students turned out to be difficult because they needed more vocabulary and background knowledge.

This Will Likely Work

An upper elementary class was writing a model paragraph together using the proper sequencing of events. The teacher suggested the class write about how to make a banana split but was surprised to learn only half of the students had eaten a banana split. She solved the problem by bringing ingredients to school the next day and making a peanut butter and jelly sandwich in front of the class. After observing the teacher, it was much easier for the class to write a model paragraph together about making a peanut butter and jelly sandwich. After this shared experience, students were then ready to write paragraphs describing a sequence of events on their own—with their own topic. This shared scaffolding and modeling is critical for ELLs. Too often, teachers ask students to write on personalized topics too soon, before they've had shared experiences.

This Likely Won't Work

In a class discussion, the teacher was trying to think of an example to help her students, so she asked, "How many of you have seen *Mission Impossible*?" Just three students raised their hands, but she continued to refer to the movie *Mission Impossible* and its star, Tom Cruise. The *Mission Impossible* example was relevant to the teacher, because she was old enough to have seen the movie, but not to most of her students. Another example comes from a class discussion about old times. The teacher referred to a story about Amish people that one of the reading groups had read. This was helpful for the five or six students in that particular reading group, but it wasn't relevant for anybody else in the class. Both of these discussions would have been better if the teachers had used *shared* experiences.

You can create relevant examples together with your students through shared activities such as field trips, speakers, demonstrations, video clips, read-alouds, or stories drawn from students' experiences. I once saw a powerful demonstration of the effectiveness of this in a 2nd grade social studies class. A key vocabulary word in the unit was "factory." As a visual example, the teacher showed the students a video clip about a chocolate factory. Several days later when students were discussing the key vocabulary in small groups, every single group referenced the video when defining "factory." The short video clip proved to be a valuable anchor point for students' understanding of this key term from the unit.

A LITTLE EXTRA . . .

- The research citation for the study on baseball background knowledge is listed in the references, but a short video summary is available at youtu.be/qP6qpSrr3cg.

- *In the Year of the Boar and Jackie Robinson* by Bette Bao Lord is a book aimed for a middle school audience, so if you're a middle school teacher, read it aloud to your students. Adults will enjoy it too. The author, a young immigrant, learns firsthand the importance of background knowledge–of Jackie Robinson, baseball, and many other things about America. As an adult, Lord became a successful author, government official, and activist.

Conclusion

Background knowledge is a key component of reading comprehension that's often overlooked. The ELL quoted at the beginning of this chapter who told me her classmate "don't know anything" had a good reason for her misconception. She was young herself and still learning. You, however, know better. You realize your

ELLs do know something—you just need to find out what it is and link it to what they are learning through relevant examples. Creating shared experiences to build background knowledge levels the playing field for everyone. That, in turn, helps give ELLs equal access to grade-level content, the topic of Chapter 8.

Meeting Realistic Yet Rigorous Standards

MISCONCEPTION: "OH, SO THEY DON'T SPEAK ENGLISH. THEN SHOULD I USE MY KINDERGARTEN CURRICULUM?"

Figure 8.1 shows a teacher dressed for her school's Halloween parade as Fiona from the *Shrek* movies. What could that possibly have to do with class work? *Everything*, because her school was in the midst of a reading campaign featuring *Shrek*, the book, with a schoolwide field trip to a community theater to see *Shrek*, the musical, the following week. This 4th grade teacher wasn't using a "kindergarten curriculum" as the teacher quoted at the beginning of this chapter was considering for her ELLs. Instead, she was using every opportunity—even something as simple and tangible as her Halloween costume—to help all of her students understand the book and the field trip. Often teachers do just the opposite and inadvertently make their instruction *more* difficult for their ELLs—and then blame the students, their parents, or both when concepts don't stick. Frustrated, they'll then lower standards and use the "kindergarten curriculum." Being an ELL is one explanation for a student's performance, but it doesn't have to be an excuse. This chapter will help you understand why it's in everybody's best

FIGURE 8.1 CONNECTING A COSTUME TO CONTENT

interests to meet in the "magic middle," crafting reasonable expectations for students while maintaining rigor.

The Problem with This Misconception

The kindergarten curriculum won't work—unless the ELL is in kindergarten. The myriad instructional models available for teaching ELLs—sheltered English, pull-out instructional model, push-in model, co-teaching model, dual language immersion, just to name a few—should lead us to conclude there is no one right way. That's because, demographically, ELLs appear in our classes in myriad ways. You may be concerned about a lone newcomer at basic proficiency, or more than half of the students in your class may be ELLs at various proficiency levels. What's important in all cases is that ELLs have access to the core curriculum you're already using for the rest of your students. In a Dear Colleague letter, the U.S. Department of Education and the U.S. Department of Justice (2015) set out ELLs' legal rights to the core curriculum. It directed schools to provide "meaningful access to all curricular and extracurricular programs" (p. 17), including gifted and talented programs and other advanced courses and programs. It also cautioned against unnecessary segregation of ELLs.

Specialized newcomer programs like the ones I taught in for my own school district pass muster as long as they are of limited duration and are voluntary. I had evidence of the good work being done in my district's newcomer programs, but even I had to admit they kept ELLs separated from mainstream classes for too long. Later, as part of a new model—school-based ESL teachers working together with general education teachers—I saw firsthand how ELLs, even newcomers, benefited from being in general education classrooms. I was convinced, and I hope I can also convince you, a classroom teacher, that ELLs belong in your classroom. Interestingly, the Every Student Succeeds Act (ESSA) is focusing on ELLs even more than its predecessor, No Child Left Behind, did. In addition to all the accountability measures of No Child Left Behind, ESSA requires states to include ELLs' progress toward proficiency as part of their reporting systems (U.S. Department of Education, 2016). This attention is a good thing for ELLs because it ensures their progress, or lack of progress, is monitored. Acquiring English language proficiency is a long process, but focusing on growth as well as achievement, in both the short and the long terms, can help ELLs succeed over time.

Read the following excerpt of an e-mail from a colleague, a teacher who believed all her 5th graders could master rigorous academic standards. She was desperate to help one of her 5th grade ELLs do so. Can you pinpoint the issues behind her question?

> Marco is STRUGGLING in class. He tries, but he has missed so much information since 1st grade that he can't attach information to what he has already learned, because unfortunately, he has not learned much. What suggestions do you have for me, Barbara? . . . He is definitely a slow learner, and . . . he has not been able to learn the facts earlier. . . . Please help me with materials to put information into his head quickly.

When my colleague said Marco had "missed so much information since 1st grade," she was pointing out the importance of background knowledge (the subject of Chapter 7). Her concern also showed how easy it is to underestimate what ELLs, even very high intermediate ELLs like Marco, can do. Building background knowledge and teaching thematically would help Marco "attach information to what he has already learned." While I was pleased that this teacher was reaching out to me for advice about her student, I was worried that she thought I had materials that "could put information into his head quickly." Unfortunately, I had no magic worksheets. I also couldn't pull Marco out of the teacher's classroom, give him a shot of English, and then send him back to the classroom "fixed." That's not possible with any ELL, but, just like with magic worksheets, wouldn't it be easy if it were? Born in the United States, Marco had been an ELL since kindergarten. My colleague claimed he was a "slow learner," but actually, she was describing the process of acquiring academic English proficiency. Widely accepted research in language acquisition (Collier, 1987) tells us it can take from five to seven years for ELLs to reach proficiency, and Marco was no exception. I just needed to remind my colleague that students like Marco need time and appropriate instructional support.

Setting This Misconception Straight

ELLs can succeed when they have access to the core curriculum and are held to high expectations. English proficiency, however, is often mistakenly assumed to be equivalent to academic knowledge, leading to well-meaning actions that unintentionally prevent access to the core curriculum. An example is the music teacher who made the comment that appears at the beginning of this chapter. Her 5th grade ELLs were ready for 5th grade musical concepts, and music is a subject area, like art and physical education, that is less dependent on language. A kindergarten music curriculum for 5th grade ELLs wasn't necessary and wouldn't have been age appropriate anyway.

At the secondary level, such misconceptions are especially damaging because ELLs tend to be "tracked" into less challenging courses. One study of ELLs in a large California high school compared course placements of ELLs with native English speakers, former ELLs, and nonnative English speakers testing proficient upon school entry (Callahan, 2005). The study found that "[p]lacement, rather than language proficiency, predicts the low grades and the low standardized test scores of long-term ELs . . . ." Later research done with a large representative national sample (Callahan & Shifrer, 2016) reached similar conclusions.

If achieving English proficiency *requires* academic English proficiency, then long-term tracking into courses with simplified content becomes a kind of self-fulfilling prophecy of underachievement, a vicious cycle that ELLs have difficulty escaping. In addition, the ELL designation can become stigmatizing the longer students have it. This is especially critical for long-term English language learners, ELLs who have been enrolled in U.S. schools for five or more years, since these students make up over half of the ELL population in secondary schools (Office of English Language Acquisition, 2015).

What do unhelpful courses with overly simplified content look like? An example Callahan (2005) gives would be a non-college-prep science course consisting of lecture, book, and paper-and-pencil work versus a science course with laboratory work and experiments that would be more likely to develop higher-order thinking. Another example I've seen would be an upper elementary schedule that puts students into three different groups by math ability—and then keeps them in those groups for social studies and science. Policies that serve to segregate long-term ELLs equate English proficiency with academic content knowledge and use that to bar ELLs from enrolling in advanced placement (AP) courses, gifted programs, or specialized coursework until they've been reclassified.

ELLs can and should continue to learn English even as they learn academic content. An ELL in my district did exactly this when, upon entering the United States as a high school junior, she was told she didn't have a good chance to graduate on time because of a lack of credits. Undaunted, she made special efforts to have her transcripts from Iraq evaluated for credits. Even as an ELL, she still lobbied for placement in AP courses her senior year and graduated two and a half years after enrolling in high school (Wiswell, 2015). This student's experience shows that, in many settings, simply being identified as an ELL can set students off track to graduate because the designation can keep them from taking the core content classes necessary for timely graduation. Even more concerning is research on high school students in Washington state, which showed even *high-achieving* current and former ELLs were less likely to take advanced courses than never ELLs (Hanson, Bisht, & Motamedi, 2016).

So what happened to Marco, the student my colleague was describing in her e-mail? It took him seven years, but Figure 8.2 shows he reached academic English proficiency at the end of his 5th grade year.

FIGURE 8.2 WHAT REACHING PROFICIENCY LOOKS LIKE

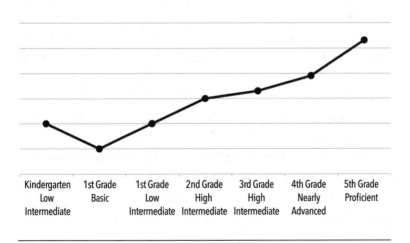

| Kindergarten Low Intermediate | 1st Grade Basic | 1st Grade Low Intermediate | 2nd Grade High Intermediate | 3rd Grade High Intermediate | 4th Grade Nearly Advanced | 5th Grade Proficient |

He spent his kindergarten year at another school before coming to my school for 1st grade. After that he moved to another school for four years. He repeated 1st grade there, and in Chapter 9 you'll learn why I would have opposed that decision had he stayed at my school. Still, he continued to make slow, steady progress during those 1st through 4th grade years until testing proficient as a 5th grader back at my school. What made the difference for Marco? First, his classroom teacher wisely reached out for help—great things can happen for students when their teachers work together. Marco's teacher learned that acquiring academic English proficiency takes time, but she still held high expectations for his progress toward proficiency. ELLs like Marco will have a realistic shot at success with teachers who believe in their ability to learn at high levels.

Making It Right in Your Classroom

It's important to understand the potential reasons for your ELLs' achievement gaps, but don't have pity. A new 3rd grade ELL at my school had received all her schooling in the United States, but her proficiency level was much lower than the other 3rd grade ELLs who had been at my school since kindergarten. I was relieved when I discovered what I thought might be one reason—the student had attended three different schools in three years. When I told the student's classroom teacher about her new ELI's academic history, she responded, "Oh, the poor baby." The teacher was concerned, which was positive, but the student needed support, not sympathy. Wanting to avoid the "*el pobrecito*" (poor thing) syndrome, I didn't agree with the teacher but instead pointed out how we could look forward to the student having a great 3rd grade year in her classroom and making lots of improvement. Understanding your ELLs' challenges doesn't mean you should expect less of them.

Digging Deeper—Differentiating Without Making Students Feel Different

The following exchange is from a video of me teaching a self-contained class of 4th and 5th grade newcomers. I'd completely forgotten this incident, but watching the video reminded me of how I was differentiating instruction on the fly for a new ELL:

> "What should he do?" asked a student as I walked by. She gestured toward the new student from Albania seated next to her. His first day in our class was already worrying her. "Tell him to copy, copy," I replied, knowing both students spoke Albanian. I pointed to the board and to the new student's paper, gave him an encouraging smile, and continued checking in with other students.

We often forget one important thing about differentiation. Even though some ELLs need instruction that's different, *they don't want to feel different.* When I told the new student to "copy, copy" the sentences other students were copying and editing, I was matter-of-factly giving him a task he could do without calling him out. I intended to collect all the students' papers, including his, to check completion. I was following the advice I often give classroom teachers—find out what your ELLs can do and then *hold them accountable for doing it.*

The students in my newcomer class often spent several weeks in general education classrooms before transferring to our district's newcomer center. After their English improved enough to describe the experience, they sometimes told me how bored and "different" they had felt in their general education classes. For example, their well-meaning teachers would park them in front of a computer for much of the day. There are many good websites for ELLs, but asking an ELL to work on a computer while the rest of the class is doing something else doesn't meet the "don't single out an ELL" test. Having an ELL do computer work when other students are doing so too is differentiating without making anybody feel different.

I deleted the video from my files after watching it this final time—no need for it now since I made it for a graduate class completed long ago. Ironically it ended up being just as useful to me later for pointing out the differentiation I was inadvertently doing. I'd recommend being more mindful about this than I was, but if you can differentiate your instruction without making your ELLs feel different, you'll be doing it in the best possible way.

Digging Deeper—Turning Less into More

We've all heard weak curriculum derided as a mile wide and an inch deep. For ELLs, depth is always better than breadth. We teachers rush to "cover" more but forget that less content in more depth creates more learning. The Common Core State Standards for math, for example, address fewer topics, but they're carefully recycled so that students are learning about them in more depth each year (Common Core State Standards Initiative, 2019b). As mentioned in Chapter 6, this actually saves time, since students won't need to relearn the same concepts every year because they had only a surface understanding of them in the first place. This applies to all subject areas, not just math.

Once, while visiting a local science museum, I met a 6th grade teacher with a class of 35 students, many of them special education students and ELLs. When I asked this teacher how she managed to give all her students what they needed, she told me she determined which key points she wanted *all* of her students to learn before she began a unit of study and then focused on those points. Her students' field trip to the museum was also a part of the unit, another indication this teacher believed in studying key points in depth. Teachers fear they're going to bore their more able students by spending more time on a topic, but they fail to recognize that studying something in depth actually encourages higher-order thinking. That engages all levels of students. The 6th grade teacher I met at the science museum understood this— less is more.

In contrast, another teacher once told me, "I don't have time," to explain why she hadn't shown a short video clip to support a social studies topic her students were studying. This teacher didn't understand that giving students the opportunity to access the content in multiple ways actually *speeds up* learning. Teachers who "don't have time" confuse covering a topic with students actually learning about it. Ironically, rushing from topic to topic and activity to activity to get everything "covered" wastes time because the learning doesn't stick when teaching is done once over lightly.

Another good way to save time is through *integration*, linking various subject areas together through a common theme. Integration among secondary classrooms, if it happens at all, takes a lot of planning and preparation among subject-area teachers. It should be easier to link subject areas together in self-contained elementary classrooms, but it's not as common as it should be. With careful integration, topics can be studied in more depth in less time.

Integration also saves time when you make an activity do linguistic double duty; students get inconspicuous correction as well as valuable practice. To illustrate how it's *not* done, here is an exchange from a typical morning meeting in a lower elementary classroom:

> **Teacher:** What did everybody do over the weekend?
> **Student:** I was sick, so I got shot yesterday.
> **Teacher:** You mean you went to the doctor and got a shot?
> **Student:** Yes.

The grammar error the student made in this conversation had the potential to impede communication because it confused the listener; the teacher was wise to correct it. The problem, however, is that the teacher is the one who gets practice saying the expression correctly, not the student. Here is a better way this exchange might occur:

> **Teacher:** What did everybody do over the weekend?
> **Student:** I was sick, so I got shot yesterday.
> **Teacher:** You mean you went to the doctor and got a shot?
> **Student:** Yes.
> **Teacher:** Can you say the whole sentence again?
> **Student:** I went to the doctor and got a shot.

In the preceding version, the teacher models the correction while the student gets feedback and then has the opportunity to practice too.

Here's another exchange that lets the student off the hook, linguistically:

> **Teacher:** What did everybody do over the weekend?
> **Student:** I went on the rides at the park on Saturday at the, the, the, the . . .
> **Teacher:** You mean the festival at the park?
> **Student:** Yeah.

Again, the teacher, not the student, says the difficult vocabulary word.

In the adapted exchange below, everybody in the class gets practice saying the unfamiliar word. In addition, the teacher also asks a follow-up question to give another student practice using the unfamiliar word:

> **Teacher:** What did everybody do over the weekend?
> **Student:** I went on the rides at the park on Saturday, the, the, the . . .
> **Teacher:** You mean the festival at the park?
> **Student:** Yeah.
> **Teacher:** Can you say it again?
> **Student:** I went on the rides at the festival at the park.
> **Teacher:** Sounds like you had fun! Everybody, say "festival."

All students: Festival.

Teacher: Yes, a festival is a happy time when people get together. Did anybody else go to the festival at the park over the weekend?

These examples illustrate how easy it is for teachers to supply language for ELLs without giving them a chance to recast their sentences. If students get practice using difficult words and phrases correctly, it will increase their chances of remembering them. A review of research on vocabulary learning for the National Reading Technical Assistance Center concluded that "[r]epetition and multiple exposures to vocabulary items are important" (Butler et al., 2010, p. 1), but opinion varies on how many exposures students need to learn unfamiliar vocabulary—15–20 exposures are often suggested, but mastery also depends on the variety and quality of the exposures, as well as the spacing between the exposures.

I found this out once when a helicopter from a local news station visited the school where I was teaching newcomers. In the week before the helicopter's visit, I read stories about helicopters aloud to my class. The students made paper "helicopters" and practiced dropping them from high places on the school's playground equipment. After watching the helicopter from the TV station land on our school's playground, the students also wrote simple thank-you letters to the news team. Several months later, one of the items on a vocabulary assessment I was administering to a student happened to be a helicopter. When I pointed to the picture and asked, "What is this?" the student sheepishly, and incorrectly, answered, "A plane?" Why in the world, I wondered, did the student forget the vocabulary word after all those exposures plus *seeing a real helicopter*? It was probably because there hadn't been any follow-up afterward. The index card activity I described in Chapter 6 would have been a good way to continue to review, but unfortunately, I wasn't wise enough at that point in my career to use it. This is why I can confidently say from my own experience that we teachers almost never give students enough exposures to new vocabulary words and opportunities to practice using them. Keep this in mind if you're wondering why your ELLs aren't retaining vocabulary and other information—once over lightly isn't enough.

Teachers sometimes hesitate to provide feedback during discussions because they are concerned that students will then be fearful of participating. Noted second-language researcher Stephen Krashen (1981) has warned that too much error correction impedes communication because it can raise ELLs' affective filter (the doubt, fears, and anxiety students might have about using a new language). However, most teachers I've watched lead discussions had the trust of their students, and everybody wanted to participate. The affective filter was low. In this case, error correction is important, especially for errors that can cause confusion to the listener or embarrassment on the part of the speaker. ELLs will never know otherwise if, for example, they're allowed to consistently use incorrect verb tenses ("I seen this," "Yesterday I go to the store") or mistake oral recess English for formal written English ("How do you spell 'gonna'?" or "I fell and hurt my booty").

I once observed a good example of a missed opportunity for error correction during a series of Monday morning meetings when students talked about what they had done over the weekend. An advanced ELL student from India, a big American football fan, always said something like, "I watched the Dallas Cowboys play a football match" or "I saw the Super Bowl match yesterday." When I asked the classroom teacher why he hadn't corrected the student, he said, "Oh, he can say it any way he wants to." The teacher probably meant to be tolerant of errors because he didn't want to raise his students' affective filter, but he didn't realize how comfortable his students were in his class. He was, in fact, missing an opportunity to change his morning meeting into a valuable language learning experience. He could have pointed out that in the United States it's an "American football game" or a "baseball game," while in other parts of the world they say a "European football match" or a "cricket match." He could even have asked the student about games played in India, such as cricket, possibly eliciting some cultural background knowledge. After I took the student aside and explained "match" versus "game" to him, he consistently reported watching American football *games* during subsequent Monday morning meetings. Error correction works, and it doesn't have to stifle communication or take up time.

Integration can either save time or waste it.

Saving Time with Integration

Lower elementary students were learning the song "Frosty the Snowman" in music class. Their classroom teacher realized many students didn't know the story behind the song. She read the story aloud to the students and showed them a short video. Singing along with the video while reading the words on a screen turned the song from music class into a valuable integrated literacy activity. In the same way, students in music class should always have access to the words of the songs they are singing. It's a great way to effortlessly integrate reading with music.

Wasting Time with Integration

"Oh, the other teacher does writing. I do grammar," said a teacher who didn't realize the best way to teach grammar is in context, through actual writing. The students in this teacher's class were doing grammar exercises like these:

Copy each sentence. Draw a line between the complete subject and complete predicate. Example: Mr. Garcia / traveled on the Amazon River.
1. His friend pointed out turtles and alligators.
2. Other passengers spotted colorful birds.
3. One of the birds squawked.
4. Another boat passed by.
5. Mr. Garcia and the other passengers waved.

The sentences actually make up a paragraph, but since they're in a numbered list, it's hard to notice they're even connected. Students would be able to comprehend the passage more easily if the sentences were presented in paragraph form, an authentic context. Still, even in paragraph form, the passage sounds stilted and contrived—not like "real" writing. It would be better to embed grammar instruction into other writing students are doing. Students need to understand subjects and predicates so that they can write complete sentences. They already do a great job of creating incomplete sentences without subjects or predicates in their own writing. Using *their* examples to teach grammar points would be much more relevant and easily understood than anything in grammar worksheets. Having students write for other content areas they are studying—in other words, integrating the subjects they're studying—saves time and enhances understanding.

A LITTLE EXTRA . . .

A visitor from a local arts organization once mistakenly asked me, "Are you the enrichment teacher?" She probably thought this because I was facilitating an arts-related project with a class that had many ELLs. This is a great way to think of an English language acquisition teacher, especially since enrichment can benefit ELLs at all proficiency levels. Following are some ways I've provided extra help:

- Made phone calls to ELL parents
- Attended parent–teacher conferences together with the classroom teacher
- Arranged and helped chaperone field trips
- Loaned bilingual books, shared video links, and suggested other resources
- Assisted ELLs with special projects

Your ESL specialist is your language "enrichment teacher" and can assist in even more ways as long as you say the magic words, "Can you help me?"

Conclusion

So, what happened with the music teacher quoted at the beginning of this chapter who was wondering about using a kindergarten curriculum with upper elementary newcomers? We got band instruments into the hands of these new ELLs, and with the music teacher's support, they participated in 5th grade band and played in school and district concerts just like every other 5th grade student. That, in a nutshell, is how to provide ELLs access to the core curriculum. ELLs need to be in mainstream classes because schools have a legal obligation to provide access to the core curriculum and activities. It's also the smart thing to do because ELLs *can* access grade-level curriculum with support. Integration and studying topics in depth can provide the recycling of vocabulary and concepts that ELLs need for mastery. Holding ELLs to high expectations is the best way to help them achieve. In the next chapter, you'll learn how to tell the difference between realistic high expectations and unrealistic hurried ones.

High Expectations Versus Hurried Expectations

MISCONCEPTION: "HE CAN'T DO THE WORK."

The quote at the beginning of this chapter isn't a misconception at all. The observation by a general education teacher about a 5th grade ELL she was recommending for retention *was* accurate. The student, in fact, couldn't do the work. The real misconception was around the teacher's reasons for this situation and the remedies to it. It is the result of moving too far away from the misconception discussed in Chapter 8: going too easy on ELLs and slowing their growth by not making their education rigorous enough. In this chapter, we'll expand on that idea and get a sense of what it looks like when we move a bit too far beyond the "magic middle" discussed in Chapter 8 and end up at the other extreme, making unreasonable demands on ELLs. This chapter covers what brings balance to this delicate equation. Specifically, I'll show you how research on time to proficiency for ELLs is often overlooked when considering student retention, a hurried expectation if there ever was one. The chapter also addresses issues with placement of ELLs at the secondary level. You will learn why you need to give your ELLs time and how much time is enough.

The Problem with This Misconception

The teacher's observation (the quote at the beginning of this chapter) was accurate but not very perceptive. High expectations for all students are a good thing, but hurried expectations are quite another. Today, it seems, kindergarten is the "new 1st grade," high school students can graduate with enough college credits to qualify as college sophomores, and teachers often teach with an eye on next year's grade-level standards instead of this year's. This hurrying can be harmful to students, but for ELLs it's especially damaging. Slow down and teach in the present; it's a marathon, not a sprint! We just keep forgetting that. The right kind of teacher expectations can contribute to ELLs' success, and that depends on looking at their progress in the *long term*. Are you aligning your expectations to your students' developmental needs as well as to the curriculum? In other words, are your expectations high or just hurried?

Setting This Misconception Straight

As I pointed out in earlier chapters, mastering academic English takes time. Figure 9.1 represents this point visually. In the top photo, I'm assessing a kindergarten student's English language proficiency; in the bottom photo, I'm assessing the same student four years later. We're both older and wiser, but he really made those four years count, testing English proficient as a 4th grader. All ELLs will improve as they get older, with progress being faster at younger ages and lower proficiency levels (WIDA Consortium, 2018); the key point is whether ELLs improve enough to catch up to their grade-level peers. Research I've done at my own school confirms this happens, given time. A group of 16 ELLs who started kindergarten and remained at my school through 5th grade scored at either an advanced or a proficient level by the end of 5th grade, even though more than half of them had scored at

FIGURE 9.1 FOUR YEARS OF PROGRESS

the low intermediate or basic level as they left kindergarten. Their worried lower elementary teachers had said they were "so low," and they *were* low—because they were still learning English. As my long-term local research showed, achieving proficiency took time and appropriate supports along the way.

National research illustrates this too. Using 12 years of data from the National Assessment of Educational Progress, Kieffer and Thompson (2018) showed that multilingual students have been making more progress than previously thought, in contrast to the relatively flat scores for all students nationally. Their study concluded that simply comparing ELLs' performance relative to that of non-ELLs doesn't give us a complete picture of the "hidden progress" of multilingual students, defined as students who reported "people in their home talk to each other in a language other than English . . . most or all of the time." This group included ELLs, former ELLs, and students from multilingual homes who had tested English proficient when they entered kindergarten. Over a 12-year period, the scores of these multilingual students in grades 4 and 8 on the NAEP reading and math assessments improved two to three times more than those of monolingual students. This is a more accurate portrayal of progress than simply looking at the performance of ELLs.

As I pointed out in Chapter 6, ELL status is not static. As ELLs reach proficiency and leave the ELL ranks, new ELLs replace them. The assessment performance gap between groups of ELLs and non-ELLs is, in effect, the gap "that can't go away" (Saunders & Marcelletti, 2013). Expecting it to narrow significantly is a good example of a hurried, unrealistic expectation. Better ways to gauge progress are to (1) include former ELLs with ELLs when assessing growth, (2) compare the performance of former ELLs with never ELLs, or (3) follow cohort groups of ELLs, the way I did at my school. All of these options require tracking students' long-term progress. This is difficult but necessary if you want to form high expectations for your ELLs, not hurried ones.

Making It Right in Your Classroom

"This is Ms. Gottschalk," said an ELL as he introduced me to his new 3rd grade classmate. "She makes things easy for people." I have yet to find a better job description for a teacher of ELLs—or any teacher, for that matter—than this one. No doubt, you too want to "make things easy for people," but first, it's important to determine whether these "things" are realistic high expectations—or unrealistic hurried ones. Figure 9.2 shows some contrasting examples.

**FIGURE 9.2 EXAMPLES OF HURRIED EXPECTATIONS
AND HIGH EXPECTATIONS**

Hurried Expectations	High Expectations
1. Why doesn't this student entering kindergarten know her letters and sounds?	1. Is this student comfortable and happy coming to school?
2. Why aren't all of my kindergarten students reading at the end of the year?	2. Why aren't all of my *developmentally ready* students reading by the end of kindergarten?
3. Rafi didn't make as much progress this year as last year.	3. Rafi didn't make as much progress this year as he did last year, but students rarely progress on an even upward trend.
4. Let's start the high school day early so that students have time for work or extracurricular activities after school.	4. Let's make the start of the school day later for teenagers. Research says they perform better with later high school start times (Owens, 2014).
5. We're doing _____ to get students ready for middle school/high school/college.	5. The best way to help students get ready for next year is to help them reach this year's age-appropriate, grade-level standards.
6. Feedback to a parent: "He's not reading at grade level."	6. Feedback to a parent: "He's not reading at grade level, but he came to the United States just two years ago. He's been making steady progress since then and is on track to catch up completely in a few more years."
7. High school ELLs with limited or interrupted formal schooling should graduate in four years with their cohorts.	7. Four years isn't enough. High school ELLs with limited or interrupted formal schooling should have the time and supports they need to graduate. High schools shouldn't be penalized for giving them the time to do so.
8. ELLs should be reading at grade level by third grade.	8. Third grade ELLs have had just four years of ELL instruction, still not long enough, since it takes five to seven years, on average, to reach proficiency. Third grade reading laws should allow retention exemptions for all ELLs.

A final example is the "goals of kindergarten" shown in Figure 9.3 from a kindergarten teacher in the 1960s. Note how the circled goals are the tangible, easily measured ones, proving teachers and students have always been subject to test pressure. It's telling to compare these standards from nearly 60 years ago to a typical Common Core State Standard for kindergarten: "Read emergent-reader texts with purpose and understanding" (CCSS.ELA-Literacy. RF.K.4). Expectations for kindergarten have changed dramatically, but children haven't. Expecting all children to meet them before they're developmentally ready is akin to expecting that children can grow all their permanent teeth faster if they just try harder and their parents work with them more at home. I once asked a kindergarten

FIGURE 9.3 GOALS OF KINDERGARTEN, CIRCA 1960s

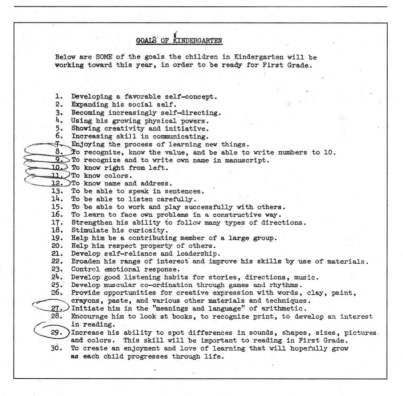

GOALS OF KINDERGARTEN

Below are SOME of the goals the children in Kindergarten will be working toward this year, in order to be ready for First Grade.

1. Developing a favorable self-concept.
2. Expanding his social self.
3. Becoming increasingly self-directing.
4. Using his growing physical powers.
5. Showing creativity and initiative.
6. Increasing skill in communicating.
7. Enjoying the process of learning new things.
8. To recognize, know the value, and be able to write numbers to 10.
9. To recognize and to write own name in manuscript.
10. To know right from left.
11. To know colors.
12. To know name and address.
13. To be able to speak in sentences.
14. To be able to listen carefully.
15. To be able to work and play successfully with others.
16. To learn to face own problems in a constructive way.
17. Strengthen his ability to follow many types of directions.
18. Stimulate his curiosity.
19. Help him be a contributing member of a large group.
20. Help him respect property of others.
21. Develop self-reliance and leadership.
22. Broaden his range of interest and improve his skills by use of materials.
23. Control emotional response.
24. Develop good listening habits for stories, directions, music.
25. Develop muscular co-ordination through games and rhythms.
26. Provide opportunities for creative expression with words, clay, paint, crayons, paste, and various other materials and techniques.
27. Initiate him in the "meanings and language" of arithmetic.
28. Encourage him to look at books, to recognize print, to develop an interest in reading.
29. Increase his ability to spot differences in sounds, shapes, sizes, pictures and colors. This skill will be important to reading in First Grade.
30. To create an enjoyment and love of learning that will hopefully grow as each child progresses through life.

teacher if students should be learning to read in kindergarten. She wisely pointed out that *some* of her kindergarten students were ready to learn to read in kindergarten, just not *all* her kindergarten students. These heightened expectations, and hurried ones for some students, can be especially damaging for ELLs whose first school experience in English might be kindergarten.

When your ELLs struggle, how can you tell whether your expectations for them are high or hurried? A good place to start is with your students' scores on your state's annual test of English language proficiency. These assessments come with descriptors telling you what ELLs at each proficiency level in each grade are able to do in each domain—listening, speaking, reading, and writing. I've found that giving classroom teachers these descriptors for their ELLs can be a revelation. A 2nd grade teacher, for example, may expect ELLs to produce grade-level argument writing by "comparing and contrasting important points and details presented in two texts on the same topic," a Can Do writing descriptor for students at full proficiency level (WIDA Consortium, 2016). What this teacher's ELLs can do independently based on their English proficiency, however, may be "indicating preferences through labeled pictures" if they're at a basic proficiency level or "describing pros and cons related to social issues or familiar topics" if they're at an intermediate level. It doesn't mean the teacher can't have ELLs "compare and contrast important points and details presented in two texts on the same topic" (the more difficult Can Do descriptor), but it does mean the teacher will need to provide more support for ELLs at lower proficiency levels. Often ELLs will have strengths and weaknesses depending on the domain. For example, one year nearly all the ELLs at my school scored lower in speaking compared to other domains. This was powerful evidence to recommend more speaking activities in general education classrooms. Knowing the descriptors for your ELLs' proficiency levels at each domain will help you craft high, not hurried, expectations for your students. It will also help you understand how much support your ELLs will need to complete assignments.

ELLs should be placed at an age-appropriate grade level when they enter U.S. schools. Trust this has been done, but still verify by confirming birth dates of your students, especially those who are struggling. While teaching in my district's magnet program for newcomers, I once discovered a student a full year younger than she should have been for her grade. Her teacher the previous year hadn't noticed it either. The fact that the student had been at a newcomer center (long since disbanded) for *nearly two years* is a good example of how easily ELLs can end up being segregated for too long. Grade placement for newcomers was done in my district at the central office. Once someone there made the inaccurate placement, everybody down the road just assumed it was correct. In this case, it wasn't. Placement at both elementary and secondary levels is often complicated because ELLs have complex educational backgrounds and can enroll at any time in the school year. This is why it's especially important for everyone involved with student registration to be properly trained and for teachers always to double-check their students' records.

Many states now have 3rd grade reading laws, as they're commonly called, which are good examples of how policy can conflict with language acquisition research—classic cases of hurried expectations. According to the National Conference of State Legislatures, 16 states and Washington, D.C. currently require retention in 3rd grade if students haven't reached a certain proficiency level (Weyer, 2018). Eight other states allow retention but don't require it. As I've pointed out in previous chapters, it can take from five to seven years for ELLs to reach academic English proficiency, especially if they start from the basic level, so considering an ELL for retention after, at most, four years of schooling, is a hurried expectation. It also violates an ELL student's rights. According to federal law, students may not be retained at grade level solely for having limited proficiency in English. The Supreme Court's decision in *Lau v. Nichols* (1974) made it clear that students with limited English proficiency must be granted equal opportunity in education and may not be discriminated against because of their lack of English. They can't be treated differently from other students (for example, kept from being promoted to the next grade) because of their lack of English language skills. U.S. Department of Education Office for Civil Rights data show that nearly 348,000 students in grades K–5 were retained in 2013–14; 18 percent of them were ELLs, far in excess of their percentage of the total school population (Office for Civil Rights 2013–14a). That's concerning. The problem with 3rd grade reading laws and similar initiatives is that they fail to acknowledge English language acquisition is developmental. Short-term, targeted reading interventions won't quickly lead to grade-level English proficiency; it takes time. As noted in Chapter 8, the last thing ELLs need is watered-down curriculum or retention with another year of the same-old, same-old. Instead, they need supports and continued access to the grade-level curriculum.

If you live in a state with a 3rd grade reading law that includes retention, there's nothing you can do about it within your classroom. What you can do, however, is understand how it affects ELLs and advocate for better supports earlier in the process—for example, ensuring ELLs have access to good-quality prekindergarten, before- and after-school programs, and summer school. If you live in a state that has no such law, you still need to understand how retention affects ELLs so that you can make wise decisions about your students. Little research on the effects of retention on ELLs, specifically, has been done, so the best we can do is extrapolate retention outcomes from students who share many of the same characteristics with ELLs. Apart from the socioemotional drawbacks, retention has not resulted in many positive academic outcomes, especially in the long term. If positive results came in the first year after retention, they faded in later years (Moser, West, & Hughes, 2012; Schwerdt, West, & Winters, 2017). This phenomenon probably explains why many classroom teachers continue to believe in retention. A teacher who recommends retention for an ELL hears later from a colleague that the retained 1st grade ELL is "doing better" in the second year of 1st grade and concludes she made the right decision. Unfortunately, teachers are far less likely to hear about the short-term benefits fading away later.

Digging Deeper—Context

Just as it's important to put ELLs' progress toward proficiency into context to determine whether expectations are high or hurried, it's also important to put what ELLs are learning into context. Decontextualized content creates all kinds of problems for ELLs, mainly because language derives its meaning from context. Context even drives how students understand things—they may have a context, but it's not the same as yours. A teacher once told me an ELL was confused about what a "pickle" was. After doing an image search with the student online, it turned out, in fact, he did understand— it was just that pickles in his home country, India, meant drumstick pickles and mango pickles usually eaten with rice. The teacher thought of pickles as dill pickles eaten with hamburgers. The ELL understood the concept but in a different, not wrong, context.

Another example of how context makes a difference linguistically is from a lower elementary class. The students were going to write letters to Miguel, the student of the day, telling him what they thought was special about him. Miguel donned headphones and got started on his computer "treat" time at the back of the classroom. Meanwhile, the teacher gathered the rest of the students to the front of the room and put the following sentence stem on the board:

Dear Miguel,

You are special because _____.

As the students talked about Miguel, the teacher wrote a few examples on the board:

Likes to play at recess

Makes me laugh

These "helpful" examples, however, were talking *about* Miguel; the students were going to write a letter *to* Miguel. The teacher would be disappointed if students wrote something like "You are special because likes to play at recess" in their letters, but the sentence stem and phrase bank were setting up students to misunderstand. A more contextualized method would be to first have students talk *about* Miguel. When it was time to write some example phrases, the teacher could help the students shift the point of view for the writing by saying: "We've been talking about Miguel. Now let's write *to* Miguel. Fadi said Miguel likes to play at recess. How would we write this if we were writing *to* Miguel? Yes, that's right. We'd say, 'You are special because you like to play at recess.'" The board work would look like this:

Dear Miguel,

You are special because you _____

like to play at recess.

make me laugh.

This kind of sentence stem and phrase bank helps students successfully write their own sentences. By being mindful of the context of the discussion and subsequent letter, the teacher could effortlessly point out language features like point of view that ELLs might not notice.

This Will Likely Work

When discussing student writing, a teacher used actual examples of student papers to illustrate common errors. With the students' permission, she used a document camera to project their papers onto the white board. She read the papers aloud and, in turn, had the rest of the students in the class discuss what was clear and what needed to be changed. When questions inevitably came up, the author was in the room and could respond. Consulting the writer of each paper gave context and thus meaning to this activity. The teacher had a trusting relationship with her students and handled the critiques with care, so students were eager to have their papers shared. They were open to revising and editing their papers after peer feedback, too, maybe even more so than after teacher feedback. Providing context when talking about a piece of writing makes revision much richer.

This Likely Won't Work

Here's an example of typical "bell work" students do at the beginning of the school day while teachers take attendance and do lunch count:

Is the subject or predicate underlined?

1. Maria and Jason <u>threw a surprise party for their mother</u>.

   _____

2. The <u>great Barrier Reef</u> is 1,250 miles long.

   _____

Correct these sentences.

3. helen keller was learned how to use sign language
   when she was for

4. the elephant drawed water in using his trunk he sprayed
   it on his back

Notice the lack of context. One sentence is about Maria and Jason, another is about the Great Barrier Reef, still another about Helen Keller, and the last sentence is about an elephant. If the teacher wanted the students to get authentic editing practice, it would make more sense to use a paragraph out of a text the students had already read or a paper one of the students had already written.

This, Too, Will Likely Work

As an alternative to out-of-context bell work, Jane Bell Kiester (1997), in her book *Caught'ya! Grammar with a Giggle*, reminds us that even simple editing exercises can be contextualized and customized to students' needs and interests. You might think this takes extra time, but it's not any more work than copying countless editing worksheets. Instead of fragmented bell work, Kiester advises giving students two or three sentences every day to copy, edit, and analyze for vocabulary. A key difference is the sentences are part of an ongoing story. Here's an example my students saw on the board on the first day I used this activity:

> once upon a time, there was a wonderful class at angus Elementary School, sixteen students where in this great class. Ms. G. and Mrs david taught this excellent student (nine mistakes)

I correctly read the sentences aloud while students copied them and then corrected the mistakes. After most students were finished, we discussed the corrections, and students made any necessary changes on their papers. Students kept their papers as two sentences were added to the story each day. As the story progressed, different characters appeared and interacted with the students. They visited places they had studied in social studies, did experiments they had done in science, and used new vocabulary words the class had learned. In the process, students learned about text features and the mechanics of writing in context. Customizing the sentences to the students built interest, and the ongoing story had meaning because it was connected to what the students were studying the rest of the day. Similarly, adding context like this to other activities your students are doing can increase their value and improve your students' understanding.

This, As Well, Likely Won't Work

"Ms. Gottschalk, what does 'tide' mean?" This question by a 2nd grade ELL encapsulates everything wrong about a hallowed tradition in many elementary classrooms—the Friday spelling test. The students' spelling words for the week all followed the same pattern: tide, hide, ride, and so on. They had a phonics context, but no meaning context, and not enough time was spent helping students understand what the words meant. That time would be less necessary, however, if spelling words were presented in context or if students were learning to spell words they wanted to use in their own writing. A common homework assignment for the weekly spelling list is to write each word several times and use each word in a sentence. Neither of these activities is contextualized. To combat unmotivated sentences ("I looked up adhesive in the dictionary.") or awkward sentences ("My friend is adhere."), teachers have concocted guidelines. Here's an example that I've seen in more than one classroom:

1. Sentences must start with a capital and end in punctuation.
2. You may not start any two sentences with the same word.
3. You may not start your sentences with the words a, I, it, my, me, we, they, he, she, the, but, and, because.
4. Each sentence must be at least nine words.
5. Each sentence must make sense.

Ironically, these guidelines break rules in the second, fourth, and fifth examples. Imagine how difficult it would be for ELLs to follow these directives using words they don't know well. The fifth example—each sentence must make sense—is especially problematic. What "makes sense" to an ELL might be very different from what sounds right to a native speaker of English. Students learning English can't rely on their intuition; they need lots

A LITTLE EXTRA . . .

Interested in using social media for professional development? I suggest following these two ELL teachers on Twitter: Judie Haynes (@judiehaynes) for elementary ELL issues and Larry Ferlazzo (@Larryferlazzo) for everything about secondary ELLs.

of context and many examples to develop a feeling for what "makes sense." Students using these guidelines with freestanding vocabulary words will, at best, produce dead language; in the worst case, they'll produce dead wrong language. Neither outcome is good. Give students context for what they're learning, and the high expectations you have for them might seem a lot less hurried.

Conclusion

This chapter should orient you to striking a balance between giving ELLs the critical patience and rigor they need to succeed. Remember, students *can* meet high, realistic expectations with the kind of support described in previous chapters. The key is recognizing hurried expectations and realizing your ELLs may struggle, but they can meet high expectations—with time. Armed with this knowledge, you are now ready to navigate another difficult topic: determining whether special education is an option to be considered—carefully—for struggling ELLs.

10

When ELLs Struggle: Special Teaching or Special Education?

MISCONCEPTION: "SHE HAS TO BE IN SCHOOL IN THE UNITED STATES FOR THREE YEARS TO QUALIFY FOR SPECIAL EDUCATION."

Did you turn to this chapter right away because you have a specific ELL in mind? Are you wondering whether that student needs special teaching or special education? Many people have addressed this question, and none of them said answering it was easy. This chapter will distill some of the most relevant information on the issue. You'll learn some common myths about the intersection of second-language development and special education placement. You'll also get practical tips on avoiding common pitfalls of over- and underidentifying ELLs for special education services.

The Problem with This Misconception

If you did, in fact, turn to this chapter first because you're wondering whether an ELL's difficulty is language learning or something else, go back and read the other chapters first. The misconceptions discussed earlier in this book can also drive inappropriate decisions about special education placement. The "three years" referenced in the misconception presented in the beginning of this chapter, like portions of the other misconceptions in this book, is partially accurate. The "wait and see" approach *can* be good practice. The WIDA Consortium (2007), which administers the ACCESS for ELLs English proficiency assessment to nearly two million ELLs in 37 states every year, advises gathering two years of data to determine growth and three years of data to determine growth trends. It also cautions that one single piece of data should not be used to make decisions about an ELL's proficiency. The biggest problem, then, with "three years to qualify for special education" is that it's just one data point. Identifying ELLs for special education services shouldn't have a rigid time-served requirement like the one referenced in this chapter's misconception. It would be a lot easier if the process were that cut and dried!

If it can be determined that ELLs truly need special education services, they should get them, no matter what their English proficiency is or how long they've been in the United States. At the same time, some ELLs may need special help, but that doesn't necessarily mean they are best served in special education. You may be wondering, what's so wrong with ELLs being overidentified for special education? After all, they'll be getting more help. It's wrong because the wrong kind of help is—unhelpful. ELLs incorrectly identified for special education will be pulled from general education classrooms to spend time in special education working on "deficits" that really aren't deficits at all but rather the process of language acquisition. By contrast, the danger of underidentification is students don't get the help they need. In other words, it seems as if *we'll never get it right*. I'm still haunted by recommendations I helped make as part of a referral team, wondering whether the decisions were correct for students. This chapter will help you get closer to making the right kinds of special education decisions for your ELLs.

Setting This Misconception Straight

If you've arrived at this chapter after reading the rest of this book, you've already taken a huge step toward setting this misconception straight. One of the biggest reasons ELLs are over- or underidentified is that the people making the decisions don't clearly understand second-language acquisition. Special education considerations are complex; I have yet to read anything on this topic that says otherwise. A child study team is made up of competent professionals, all knowledgeable in different fields but, unfortunately, not in all fields. However, even if you could create and then clone the perfect child study team member by combining a psychologist, a speech therapist, a social worker, a special education teacher, an English language acquisition teacher, and a general education teacher, all with bilingual ability in their students' home languages, it wouldn't be the best solution. A team approach, with a diversity of knowledge and backgrounds, is best.

I know I did my best work identifying ELLs for possible special education services as part of a team that had been in place for several years at the same school. I worked with professionals at the top of their game in special education, but they freely admitted they didn't know much about English language acquisition. "Barbara, what is it exactly that you do?" asked my school's new speech therapist. I was just as clueless about her field, but because we were willing to work together and, even more important, learn from each other, we were able to make the best possible decisions for ELLs.

A language acquisition professional should be part of the initial and subsequent Individualized Education Program (IEP) meetings for all ELLs. First, determine whether the student you're considering is, in fact, an ELL. Keep in mind that all ELLs are on a language acquisition teacher's radar screen, not just the ones taught in small group sessions or enrolled in ESL courses. At the same time, a student may come from a home where a language other than English is spoken, but that doesn't necessarily mean the student is an ELL. The student could be a former ELL or a student who tested proficient when entering school. The ESL teacher, along with your school counselor, is probably one of the few staff members in your school who has a long-term view of an ELL. Unlike classroom teachers who usually teach students for one year, or in the case of secondary teachers, sometimes for just one semester, an English language acquisition teacher monitors the progress of ELLs from the time they are identified until several years after they have been reclassified and are no longer receiving services. That long-term view can provide a valuable perspective. An ELL teacher will have useful information to contribute about a student's "ELL life" even if the student is nearly proficient and is only being monitored.

Making It Right in Your Classroom

Many factors should be considered when determining whether special education is appropriate for an ELL. It's especially import-ant for classroom teachers to understand these factors because they are the ones most likely to generate a special education referral. According to the National Center for Education Statistics (2018b), in 2015–16, 34 percent of all special education students had a specific learning disability, defined as "a disorder in one or more of the basic psychological processes involved in under-standing or using language, spoken or written, that may manifest itself in an imperfect ability to listen, think, speak, read, write, spell, or do mathematical calculations." Another 20 percent had speech and language impairments. Both of these disorders, which together account for more than half of the students served in special education, can be easily confused with the normal process of second-language acquisition. Misinterpretation can lead to inaccurate conclusions and wrong placements. First, consider the big picture.

Count the Students

It's useful, for starters, to know what percentage of your school's special education population are ELLs. Is it comparable to the percentage of ELLs in the general school population? In other words, is it proportionate? Nationwide, ELLs represented 10.2 percent of students served in special education and 9.9 percent of the total school population (Office for Civil Rights, 2013–14b). This appears proportionate. Morgan et al. (2015), using a large representative, multiyear dataset, consistently found no evidence of overrepresentation of language-minority schoolchildren in special education and claimed these students are underrepresented in special education. These findings may have been due to differences in how "ELL" and "language-minority student" are defined. Ethnic status and language spoken in the home don't necessarily indicate a student is an ELL. In addition, ELL status is dynamic; a special education student may be an ELL one year and a former ELL several years later. This makes simply counting the number of ELLs in special education more difficult than it appears to be on the surface. Districts identify students for special education services differently; criteria for reclassification from ELL status varies by state and district as well. The same data that return a proportionate percentage of ELLs in special education nationwide show big differences in identification rates at the state and district levels.

Using information available online from the Office for Civil Rights (2013–14b, 2013–14c), I found identification rates that varied by over 20 percentage points—even for school districts of similar size and with similar percentages of ELLs. ELLs were overrepresented in special education compared to the general population in some districts and underrepresented in others. If your school district has a large number of ELLs, other useful information could include the distribution of ELLs in special education with respect to other characteristics, such as grade level, home language, or disability category. For example, research done on a large sample of urban school districts in California (Artiles, Rueda, Salazar, & Higareda, 2005) found that ELLs at the secondary level were more likely to be overrepresented in special education than ELLs in the elementary grades. Nationwide, identification rates for most disability categories have been found to be consistent with the general population; however, identification of ELLs for specific learning disabilities, at 50 percent, was well above the rate for the general population of students, at 39 percent (IDEA Data Center, 2015, as cited in WIDA Consortium, 2017b). Your focus should always be on how to best serve individual students, but being aware of larger trends and knowing your local numbers will help. You can't determine whether you may be over- or underidentifying ELLs for special education until you actually count the students.

Check Assessments

As a general education teacher, you'll be using classroom assessment information you gather to determine whether an ELL might need special education services. Document as much you can; your insights and observations will carry more weight if they're backed up with evidence. Are the assessments you're using normed on ELLs? Even simple formative classroom assessments are subject to measurement error if they're not. For example, a perceptive staff member at my school told me she realized while she was asking 1st graders to tell her the first sound in a word that students didn't understand what "first" and "last" meant. Using results from this kind of evaluation would indicate students don't know their sounds, but, in fact, they couldn't demonstrate their knowledge because they didn't understand the assessment directions. Figure 10.1 shows another similar example, in which 1st graders were asked to write the initial consonant for each word. Pictures are a great way to *teach* initial sounds, but this assessment assumed too much. If ELLs didn't know the word for "fox" in English, for example, they wouldn't be able to supply the initial consonant in English. The teacher who used an assessment like this one might conclude a student didn't know his initial sounds when, instead, the student didn't know the *names* for the pictures. Both of the assessments in these examples were testing the wrong thing.

FIGURE 10.1 ASSESSMENT FOR INITIAL SOUNDS

____og	____est	____et	____ox

Another common miscalculation with assessments involves assuming students don't understand the language if they can't produce it, forgetting that receptive domains, such as listening, can develop faster than productive domains, such as speaking (WIDA Consortium, 2017a). I've had more proficient and perceptive ELLs tell me, "I know what you mean, but I just can't say it." I believed them. Try to structure assessments to help ELLs show you what they know. For example, my school's speech therapist advised me to set up situations to encourage a selective mute ELL to talk. Following her advice, I arranged it so that items the student needed in class were out of her reach so that she had to ask me for them. This gave me evidence that the student, in fact, could communicate her needs. Set up similar situations so that students can more easily show you what they know. If you say to a student, "Merna, please give me the scissors," and the student gives you the scissors, that's evidence of understanding. Count it.

Avoid a Deficit Viewpoint

When an ELL is struggling, consider outside factors that might be causing problems; don't assume something is wrong with the child. It's also important not to interpret normal language acquisition as language delay. For example, young ELLs sometimes switch back and forth between their two languages. Teachers might view this "code switching" as language confusion, but it's not. ELLs are simply using all the words they have—in both of their languages—to express themselves. Perceived language "problems" may also be a result of transference from the native language. For example, a Spanish-speaking child may have trouble with English vowels since English has more vowels than Spanish does; Arabic doesn't have /p/, so an Arabic-speaking ELL might say "bizza" instead of "pizza." A Chinese-speaking ELL may confuse "he" and "she" because in Chinese these forms are pronounced the same. Language transfer errors don't indicate a disability.

Because classroom teachers often don't realize where an ELL started, they can underestimate how quickly a student can become proficient. For example, when worried lower elementary teachers at my school kept telling me about students who were "so low," I reminded them these students had started kindergarten at basic proficiency levels and had, in fact, made a lot of progress. The teachers were being too hard on themselves and their students! Imagine how satisfying it was to tell these teachers the good news when their former students eventually tested proficient.

Language matters, so the wording around multitiered systems of support (MTSS) and response to intervention (RTI) is rather misleading with respect to ELLs. According to Merriam-Webster, an intervention means "the act of interfering with the outcome or course especially of a condition or process (as to prevent harm or improve functioning)," but that doesn't describe language acquisition at all. Teachers of ELLs aren't trying to interfere with anything or change the outcome of the language acquisition process;

if anything, they're trying to accelerate it. They're also not aiming instruction at a particular weakness. An ELL might, for example, need to work on mastering vowel sounds or writing complete sentences, but even after that, the overall language acquisition process continues. The intention of many assessments for special education is to identify a specific weakness or disability and then remediate it. That's perfectly okay if the student has one, but there's nothing wrong with most ELLs; they're simply still learning the language.

Figure 10.2 presents factors to consider as a child is being evaluated for special education services. Keep in mind that it's not a

FIGURE 10.2   FACTORS TO CONSIDER IN EVALUATING ELLs FOR SPECIAL EDUCATION

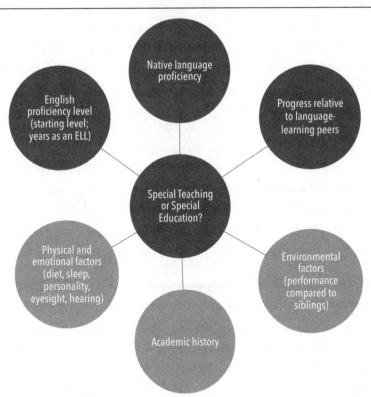

learning disability if a child's lack of progress is due to an environmental, cultural, or economic disadvantage (Individuals with Disabilities Education Act, 2004). All the factors in Figure 10.2 have an ELL component, but those in the darker circles are specific to ELLs. Let's start by addressing the three factors in lighter circles, which are important for all students—physical and emotional factors, academic history, and environmental factors—and then address the other factors—English proficiency level, native language proficiency, and progress relative to ELL peers.

Physical and emotional factors. Sometimes teachers are overly concerned about shy students or ELLs simply listening carefully before they're willing to speak, so it's important to consider a child's personality. Being introverted isn't a disability. Also consult with parents about a child's sleep habits, eating habits, and possible vision and hearing problems. Admittedly, these physical factors aren't things teachers can easily change at school, but something as simple as a child getting eyeglasses or eating better can make a big difference. Working with parents on something concrete can contribute to improvement easily.

Academic history. Academic histories are always important. Unfortunately, ELLs are more likely to have incomplete records, which makes getting a student history difficult. Academic information from the home country, if it's available, needs to be translated and evaluated. Even information supplied by parents may be incomplete or inaccurate. Mobility within the United States can also create inconsistencies in student records. My school once enrolled a new family from another school in our state with three children receiving special education services. The oldest child and the youngest child were identified as ELLs, while the middle sibling was not. To make matters even more confusing, the IEP for the non-ELL child indicated he was not limited English proficient. Technically, that was accurate, but the IEP also described the child as "bilingual" and said the family spoke Arabic. The parents told us they had simply overlooked the home language survey questions and left them blank when they registered the middle sibling for kindergarten. How this child had been identified for special education services without anybody wondering about this is anybody's guess. It's a great example, though, of how inconsistent—and confusing—a student's academic records can be.

For the ELL you're considering, note the number of schools the child has attended. Was the student's prior schooling limited or interrupted? A student's lack of progress may simply be due to missing a significant amount of school. Has the student attended several different schools in the United States? If so, what about the student's attendance record there? Are there any behaviors, such as suspensions or expulsions, that might have resulted in interrupted learning? Also, are the child's parents concerned about the student's lack of progress? Often parents want extra help for their children, so it's useful to have evidence to show how the student has been helped and whether it has worked. If parents aren't convinced special education services are needed, or if they're worried about their child being designated as "different," such evidence will prove useful.

Environmental factors. Conscientious parents avoid comparing siblings, and that's a good thing most of the time. Still, a sibling's language development history can provide useful information for a struggling ELL. Arabic-speaking twins at my school were an interesting example of this. The 1st and 2nd grade teachers of one twin referred the student for special education evaluation, while the 1st and 2nd grade teachers of the other twin didn't. The parents reported the twin being considered for special education had shown language delay in the home language, unlike the other twin. This was significant since, as twins, they had the same age and home-language background. Delay in the home language was also significant. It's more likely a true learning disability if a student's weakness is evident in both English and the home language. The students had similar results on most other assessments, but a member of the child study team pointed out that if we simply looked at test data, the decision would be cut and dried, and meetings wouldn't be necessary. The input from parents and classroom teachers in this case proved to be important. This is why informed teacher recommendations are so critical. If you're reading this book, you'll be able to make them.

English proficiency level. An ELL's English proficiency level is always relevant, especially if that student is having academic difficulties. Your state's annual test of English language proficiency (for example, WIDA ACCESS, and KELPA) is likely one of the few assessments administered to your students that has been normed for ELLs. That's why teachers need to consider the information this test gives. For example, a high school math teacher once asked her school's counselor if a Spanish-speaking student could be moved to another class section that had more Spanish speakers. The teacher, who didn't speak Spanish, told the counselor, "I just can't explain things." It's commendable the math teacher wanted to help the student and, as I've suggested in Chapter 3, a language buddy is a good first start. What's missing, though, is that neither the teacher nor the counselor knew the student's English proficiency level or how many years this student had been studying in the United States. A native language study buddy would be good support if the student in question had basic English proficiency, but what if the student had received all of his schooling in the United States and had very little academic Spanish vocabulary? A native language study buddy wouldn't help much, and even more worrisome, it might mask the student's real problems. It's important to know this information before suggesting options for students having academic difficulties, but it's essential when considering students for special education services.

Native language proficiency. It's important to assess the child's home language, if you can. If standardized bilingual assessments aren't available, at least ask the parents about the child's language development in her home language. School staff members who are bilingual in the language of the student might also be able to give you an idea of the child's home language ability. Try asking students for the home language equivalent of vocabulary words you're studying in English. This ad hoc "assessment" certainly can't take the place of a valid bilingual measure of language ability, but if ELLs don't know vocabulary in their native language, that tells you something. Even more important, if they do know, it will remind you to acknowledge both languages; a student's total language proficiency, then, might not seem so limited.

Progress relative to ELL peers. It's essential to look at a child's long-term progress relative to an ELL peer group. Where the student started is important. It seems the only time we assemble longitudinal data on students is when they are being considered for special education, but we should do this for many students. Then, we would have a better idea of what satisfactory long-term progress looks like. A teacher with a short-term viewpoint may rightly say a child is "low," but progress needs to be assessed over several years. Compare the ELL you're considering for special education to other ELLs who started at the same grade and proficiency levels. For example, once when a 3rd grade ELL was being considered for special education, I looked at the other ELLs in my district who had scored at the same level on an English language proficiency test in kindergarten as the student we were considering. When I compared these students' proficiency scores two years later, I found 75 percent had scored higher than the student in question at the end of 2nd grade. This was significant. For institutions with low numbers of ELLs, doing this will be more difficult because a large peer group won't be available for comparison. Still, student growth percentiles may be available for your state's English proficiency assessment. Comparison to ELL peers, by itself, shouldn't determine special education placement—no single piece of data should—but it is an important part of an ELL student's history.

After an ELL Is Identified and Placed in Special Education

- *Your language acquisition specialist will continue monitoring an ELL's progress and provide service if necessary.* If a student qualifies for both special education and ELL services, neither set of supports trumps the other—both should be provided if deemed necessary. A general education teacher can serve as a sort of "team leader," making sure the teachers providing special education services understand the ELL side of the student and vice versa.

- *Use clear English in the students' IEPs to make them more comprehensible to parents and easier to translate, if necessary.* Even English-speaking parents could use a translator to fully understand some IEPs. The examples in Figure 10.3 show how to improve the language of IEPs.

- *Make sure parents can fully participate in IEP meetings by translating vital written material and having an interpreter present, if necessary.* A trained, sensitive interpreter can act as a cultural broker as well as a language interpreter. My school's special education personnel tried to take advantage of the interpreters provided through our county service district mainly because these professionals had experience with IEPs and special education issues. I've learned from experience to arrange for an interpreter even if it doesn't seem necessary. Once, for an annual IEP for an ELL, an interpreter wasn't secured because the student's English-speaking father was scheduled to attend. We were surprised when, instead, the student's mother came. She spoke serviceable English, so I assumed things were going well. Still, I felt guilty when she pulled out paper and pencil from her purse and started taking notes in Arabic. We should have erred on the side of caution and arranged for an interpreter to ease the language burden on the parent. I've made phone calls using my district's telephone translation service and had the parent wave off the interpreter, telling me in English it wasn't necessary. At the time, I worried I might have offended, but isn't it better to *give the parent the power* to decide whether interpretation is necessary than not having it available when it's needed?

FIGURE 10.3 IMPROVING THE LANGUAGE OF IEPs

Language	The Problem with The Language	Improved Language
Fadi is a really sweet little boy.	Too subjective.	Fadi has many friends in class and plays with them every day at recess.
Currently Rafael has difficulty having consistent attendance, which makes progress move slowly.	Not specific.	Rafael has a 70 percent attendance rate.
It was noted that Valentina still has some confusion with the concept of *same* vs. *different*.	Wordy.	Valentina confuses *same* with *different*.
Marko is able to navigate in and out of his classroom environment without difficulty independently.	Obscure.	Marko can walk to and from the classroom on his own.
It is observed that Ronny has a difficult time getting his ideas down in complete sentences but writes fragment sentences.	Wordy.	Ronny writes in fragments, not complete sentences.
Mariam's language skills are also affected by her bilingual language experiences.	This statement seems to imply the child's bilingual ability has a negative effect on her English language skills. As you've learned in Chapter 2, this isn't true.	Omit.

A LITTLE EXTRA . . .

- The U.S. Department of Education's Office for Civil Rights gathers data from U.S. schools on access and equity issues at ocrdata.ed.gov/DistrictSchoolSearch. Here you can find your school's and district's percentages of ELLs in special education compared to ELL percentages in the general population. You can also run searches to compare your school to schools with similar percentages of ELLs.

- *The Spirit Catches You and You Fall Down: A Hmong Child, Her American Doctors, and the Collision of Two Cultures* by Anne Fadiman follows the journey of a Hmong family dealing with their child's severe epilepsy as they navigate the medical maze in America. Their story points out several cultural divides—medical versus nonmedical, Hmong versus American—with everyone trying to do their misguided best for this severely ill child. It reminded me of how many different ways we can misunderstand each other.

Conclusion

I hope this chapter has made you realize how complex identifying ELLs for special education services can be. More important, now you know the reasons. The fact that there are such big differences in proportionality when comparing schools, districts, and states indicates the process isn't easy for anybody, so it's okay if you feel that way too. The process is also different for everybody because each student you will consider is different. We can look at group identification rates and worry about proportionality, but in the end we need to consider the individual student. The best way to correctly identify ELLs for special education is to have knowledgeable members on the child study team bring their best information. Members will have their own biases (I know I did), but a team decision will work out best for the student.

Appendix

Each state has a slightly different data system for public reporting, but all states must provide a system to the public as part of ESSA requirements. As a classroom teacher, you owe it to yourself to learn how to navigate your state's data system and learn to understand the data reported in it. You also owe it to your students' parents to show them how to interpret these data so that they can understand them too. Use this table to find your state's data reporting website and to determine which English language proficiency test your state uses.

Alabama	WIDA	http://www.alsde.edu/dept/data/Pages/home.aspx
Alaska	WIDA	https://education.alaska.gov/data-center
Arizona	AZELLA	http://www.azed.gov/accountability-research/data/
Arkansas	ELPA21	https://adedatabeta.arkansas.gov/
California	ELPAC	https://www.ed-data.org/
Colorado	WIDA	https://www.cde.state.co.us/cdereval
Connecticut	LAS Links	http://edsight.ct.gov/SASPortal/main.do
Delaware	WIDA	http://profiles.doe.k12.de.us/SchoolProfiles/State/Default.aspx

District of Columbia	WIDA	https://dcps.dc.gov/service/school-data
Florida	WIDA	http://www.fldoe.org/accountability/data-sys/edu-info-accountability-services/pk-12-public-school-data-pubs-reports/
Georgia	WIDA	http://www.gadoe.org/technology-services/data-collections/Pages/Data-Collections-and-Reporting.aspx
Hawaii	WIDA	http://www.hawaiipublicschools.org/VisionForSuccess/SchoolDataAndReports/Pages/home.aspx
Idaho	WIDA	https://boardofed.idaho.gov/data-research/statistics/
Illinois	WIDA	https://www.illinoisreportcard.com
Indiana	WIDA	https://www.doe.in.gov/idoe/idoe-data
Iowa	ELPA21	https://educateiowa.gov/education-statistics
Kansas	KELPA	http://ksreportcard.ksde.org
Kentucky	WIDA	https://education.ky.gov/districts/tech/Pages/K-12-Data.aspx
Louisiana	ELPT	https://www.louisianabelieves.com/resources/library/data-center
Maine	WIDA	https://www.maine.gov/doe/data/
Maryland	WIDA	http://reportcard.msde.maryland.gov/
Massachusetts	WIDA	http://profiles.doe.mass.edu/
Michigan	WIDA	http://www.mischooldata.org
Minnesota	WIDA	https://rc.education.state.mn.us/
Mississippi	ELPT	https://www.mdek12.org/OPR/Reporting/Reports
Missouri	WIDA	https://mcds.dese.mo.gov/guidedinquiry/School Report Card/School Report Card.aspx
Montana	WIDA	http://www.alecreportcard.org/state/mt/
Nebraska	ELPA21	http://nep.education.ne.gov/
Nevada	WIDA	http://nevadareportcard.com/di/

New Hampshire	WIDA	https://www.education.nh.gov/assessment-systems/
New Jersey	WIDA	https://rc.doe.state.nj.us/
New Mexico	WIDA	http://aae.ped.state.nm.us/
New York	NYSESLAT	https://data.nysed.gov/reportcard.php?year=2017&state=yes
North Carolina	WIDA	http://www.ncpublicschools.org/accountability/reporting/
North Dakota	WIDA	https://insights.nd.gov/Data
Ohio	ELPA21	http://reportcard.education.ohio.gov/Pages/default.aspx
Oklahoma	WIDA	https://www.schoolreportcard.org/report-card
Oregon	ELPA21	https://www.oregon.gov/ode/schools-and-districts/reportcards/reportcards/Pages/default.aspx
Pennsylvania	WIDA	https://www.education.pa.gov/Data-and-Statistics/Pages/default.aspx
Rhode Island	WIDA	http://www.ride.ri.gov/Information Accountability/RIEducationData.aspx
South Carolina	WIDA	https://ed.sc.gov/data/
South Dakota	WIDA	https://doe.sd.gov/data.aspx
Tennessee	WIDA	https://www.tn.gov/education/data/data-downloads.html
Texas	TELPAS	https://tea.texas.gov/Reports_and_Data/
Utah	WIDA	https://www.schools.utah.gov/data
Vermont	WIDA	https://education.vermont.gov/data-and-reporting
Virginia	WIDA	http://www.doe.virginia.gov/statistics_reports/
Washington	ELPA21	http://www.k12.wa.us/DataAdmin/default.aspx
West Virginia	ELPA21	https://wvde.state.wv.us/data/
Wisconsin	WIDA	https://dpi.wi.gov/families-students/data
Wyoming	WIDA	https://edu.wyoming.gov/data/

Bibliography

Artiles, A., Rueda, R., Salazar, J., & Higareda, I. (2005). Within-group diversity in minority disproportionate representation: English language learners in urban school districts. *Exceptional Children, 71*(3), 283–300. Retrieved from www.kau.edu.sa/Files/0008884/Files/48501_VOLUME71NUMBER3Spring2005_EC_Artiles71-3.pdf

August, D. (Ed.). (2006). Executive summary. *Developing literacy in second language learners: Report of the National Literacy Panel on language-minority children and youth.* Hillsdale, NJ: Lawrence Erlbaum Associates. Retrieved from www.standardsinstitutes.org/sites/default/files/material/developing-literacy-in-second-language-learners-executive-summary_2.pdf

Batalova, J., & Alperin, E. (2018). *Immigrants in the U.S. states with the fastest-growing foreign-born populations.* Retrieved from www.migrationpolicy.org/article/immigrants-us-states-fastest-growing-foreign-born-populations

Butler, S., et al. (2010). *A review of the current research on vocabulary instruction.* National Reading Technical Assistance Center, RMC Research Corporation. Retrieved from www2.ed.gov/programs/readingfirst/support/rmcfinal1.pdf

Callahan, R. (2005). Tracking and high school English learners: Limiting opportunity to learn. *American Educational Research Journal, 42,* 305–328.

Callahan, R., & Shifrer, D. (2016). Equitable access for secondary English learner students: Course taking as evidence of EL program effectiveness. *Educational Administration Quarterly, 52*(3), 463–496. Retrieved from www.ncbi.nlm.nih.gov/pmc/articles/PMC4941630/

Child Trends. (n.d.). Dual language learners. Retrieved from https://www.childtrends.org/indicators/dual-language-learners

ClassDojo Blog. (2018, December 12). What we learned about teacher-family language barriers…and how one district is doing something about it [blog post]. Retrieved from blog.classdojo.com/what-we-learned-about-teacher-family-language-barriers-and-how-one-district-is-doing-something-about-it/

Collier, V. (1987). Age and rate of acquisition of second language for academic purposes. *TESOL Quarterly, 21*(4), 617–641. Retrieved from www.thomasandcollier.com/assets/age---rate-of-acquisition---.pdf

Common Core State Standards Initiative. (2019a). English language arts standards. Retrieved from www.corestandards.org/ELA-Literacy/RF/K/

Common Core State Standards Initiative. (2019b). Key shifts in mathematics. Retrieved from www.corestandards.org/other-resources/key-shifts-in-mathematics/

Cummins, J. (1999). BICS and CALP: Clarifying the distinction. ERIC document ED43855. Retrieved from files.eric.ed.gov/fulltext/ED438551.pdf

Education Commission of the States. (2014a). 50-state comparison: What ELL training, if any, is required of general classroom teachers? Retrieved from ecs.force.com/mbdata/mbquestNB2?rep=ELL1415

Education Commission of the States. (2014b). 50-state comparison: What methods are used to identify English language learners? Retrieved from ecs.force.com/mbdata/mbquestNB2?rep=ELL1403

Elementary and Secondary Education Act of 1965. (As amended by the Every Student Succeeds Act.) (2018). Section 3121. Retrieved from legcounsel.house.gov/Comps/Elementary And Secondary Education Act Of 1965.pdf

Feistritzer, C. (2011). *Profile of teachers in the U.S. 2011*. National Center for Education Information. Retrieved from www.edweek.org/media/pot2011final-blog.pdf

Genesee, F., & Riches, C. (2006). Literacy: Instructional issues. In Genesee, F., Lindholm-Leary, K., Saunders, W., & Christian, D. (Eds.), *Educating English language learners: A synthesis of research evidence*. Cambridge, UK: Cambridge University Press. Retrieved from medicine.kaums.ac.ir/uploadedfiles/files/educating_english_language_learners.pdf

Goldring, R., Taie, S., & Riddles, M. (2014). *Teacher attrition and mobility: Results from the 2012–13 teacher follow-up survey* (NCES 2014-077). Washington, DC: U.S. Department of Education, National Center for Education Statistics. Retrieved from nces.ed.gov/pubs2014/2014077.pdf

Goodenough, F. (1926). Racial differences in the intelligence of school children. *Journal of Experimental Psychology, 9*, 388–397.

Goodwin, B. (2017, September). Research matters/The power of parental expectations. *Educational Leadership, 75*(1), 80–81. Retrieved from: www.ascd.org/publications/educational-leadership/sept17/vol75/num01/The-Power-of-Parental-Expectations.aspx

Gottschalk, B. (1994). 40 helpful hints & tips for making your ESL teaching easier and more fun, *Hands-on English, 22*. Retrieved from www.handsonenglish.com/40tips.html

Hakuta, K., Butler, Y., & Witt, D. (2000). *How long does it take English learners to attain proficiency?* The University of California Linguistic Minority Research Institute Policy Report 2000-1. Stanford, CA: Stanford University. Retrieved from https://web.stanford.edu/~hakuta/Publications/%282000%29%20-%20HOW%20LONG%20DOES%20IT%20TAKE%20ENGLISH%20LEARNERS%20TO%20ATTAIN%20PR.pdf

Hanson, H., Bisht, B., & Motamedi, J. (2016, November). Advanced course enrollment and performance among English learner students in Washington state. Regional Educational Laboratory at Education Northwest, Institute of Education Sciences, U.S. Department of Education. Retrieved from files.eric.ed.gov/fulltext/ED570326.pdf

Hirsch, E.D., Jr. (2006). *The knowledge deficit: Closing the shocking education gap for American children*. Boston: Houghton Mifflin.

Individuals with Disabilities Education Act. (2004). Sec. 300.309 (a) (3). U.S. Dept. of Education, Retrieved from sites.ed.gov/idea/regs/b/d/300.309/a/3

Kieffer, M., & Thompson, K. (2018, August/September). Hidden progress of multilingual students on NAEP. *Educational Researcher, 47*(6), 391–398.

Kiester, J. (1997). *Caught'ya! grammar with a giggle*. Gainesville, FL: Maupin House.

Krashen, S. (1981). *Second language acquisition and second language learning*. Oxford, UK: Pergamon Press. Retrieved from www.sdkrashen.com/content/books/sl_acquisition_and_learning.pdf

Lau v. Nichols, 414 U.S. 563 (1974). Retrieved from caselaw.findlaw.com/us-supreme-court/414/563.html

Learning Heroes. (2018, December). *Parents 2018: Going beyond good grades*. Retrieved from https://bealearninghero.org/parent-mindsets/

Lindholm-Leary, K., & Borsato, G. (2006). Academic achievement. In Genesee, F., Lindholm-Leary, K., Saunders, W., & Christian, D. (Eds.), *Educating English language learners: A synthesis of research evidence.* Cambridge, U.K.: Cambridge University Press. Retrieved from medicine.kaums.ac.ir/uploadedfiles/files/educating_english_language_learners.pdf

Lorenz, T. (2018, September 12). Teens are protesting in-class presentations. *The Atlantic.* Retrieved from www.theatlantic.com/education/archive/2018/09/teens-think-they-shouldnt-have-to-speak-in-front-of-the-class/570061/

Marzano, R. J., Pickering, D. J., & Pollock, J. E. (2012). *Classroom instruction that works: Research-based strategies for increasing student achievement* (2nd ed.). Alexandria, VA: ASCD.

McBride, T., Nief, R., & Westerberg, C. (2018). The Mindset List for the class of 2022. Retrieved from http://themindsetlist.com/2018/08/beloit-college-mindset-list-class-2022/

Menken, K., Funk, A., & Kleyn, T. (2011). Teachers at the epicenter: Engagement and resistance in a biliteracy program for "long-term English language learners" in the U.S. In Hélot, C., & Ó Laoire, M. (Eds.), *Language Policy for the Multilingual Classroom: Pedagogy of the Possible.* Cleveldon, Avon, UK: Multilingual Matters. Retrieved from www.academia.edu/12452503/Teachers_at_the_Epicenter_Engagement_and_Resistance_in_a_Biliteracy_Program_for_Long_Term_English_Language_Learners_in_the_U.S

Michigan Center for Educational Performance and Information. (2018). *WIDA ACCESS performance: Proficiency level snapshot (2017–18).* Retrieved from www.mischooldata.org/Wida2/WidaAccess/WidaProficiencyLevel.aspx

Morgan, P. L., Farkas, G., Hillemeier, M. M., Mattison, R., Maczuga, S., Li, H., & Cook, M. (2015). Minorities are disproportionately underrepresented in special education: Longitudinal evidence across five disability conditions. *Educational Research, 44,* 278–292. Retrieved from: www.ncbi.nlm.nih.gov/pmc/articles/PMC4950880/

Moser, S. E., West, S. G., & Hughes, J. N. (2012). Trajectories of math and reading achievement in low-achieving children in elementary school: Effects of early and later retention in grade. *Journal of Educational Psychology, 104*(3), 603–621. Retrieved from www.ncbi.nlm.nih.gov/pmc/articles/PMC3547658/

National Academies of Sciences, Engineering, and Medicine. (2017). *Promoting the educational success of children and youth learning English: Promising futures.* Washington, DC: National Academies Press. Retrieved from www.nap.edu/catalog/24677/promoting-the-educational-success-of-children-and-youth-learning-english

National Assessment of Educational Progress. (2017). *The nation's report card,* Retrieved from www.nationsreportcard.gov/

National Assessment Governing Board. (2018). *Panel: A national challenge: What can be done to improve reading achievement?* NAEP Day, Release of the 2017 Nation's Report Card. Retrieved from www.nagb.gov/naep-results/reading/2017-naep-reading-and-math-report.html

National Center for Education Statistics. (2011a). Number and percentage of all public schools that had any students with an Individual Education Plan (IEP) because of special needs or formally identified disability, or who were English-language learners (ELLs) or limited-English proficient (LEP), and percentage of students with an IEP/formally identified disability or who were ELLs/LEP, by state: 2011–12. *Schools and Staffing Survey.* U.S. Department of Education. Retrieved from nces.ed.gov/surveys/sass/tables/sass1112_2013312_s2s_002.asp

National Center for Education Statistics. (2011b). Number of public school teachers and percentage of public school teachers who taught limited-English proficiency (LEP) or English language learner (ELL) students, by selected school and teacher characteristics: 2011–12. *Schools and Staffing Survey.* U.S. Department of Education. Retrieved from nces.ed.gov/surveys/sass/tables/sass1112_498_t1n.asp

National Center for Education Statistics. (2013–14). Table 1. Public high school 4-year adjusted cohort graduation rate (ACGR), by race/ethnicity and selected demographics for the United States, the 50 states, and the District of Columbia. Common Core of Data: America's Public Schools. U.S. Department of Education. Retrieved from nces.ed.gov/ccd/tables/ACGR_RE_and_characteristics_2013-14.asp

National Center for Education Statistics. (2017). Number and percentage distribution of teachers in public and private elementary and secondary schools, by selected teacher characteristics. *Schools and Staffing Survey.* U.S. Department of Education. Retrieved from nces.ed.gov/programs/digest/d17/tables/dt17_209.10.asp

National Center for Education Statistics. (2018a). Table 8. Percentage of public school teachers who took graduate or undergraduate courses before their first year of teaching in selected subject areas, by selected school characteristics: 2015–16. *Characteristics of public elementary and secondary school teachers in the U.S.: Results from the 2015–16 National Teacher and Principal Survey.* U.S. Department of Education. Retrieved from nces.ed.gov/pubs2017/2017072rev.pdf

National Center for Education Statistics. (2018b). Children and youth with disabilities. U.S. Department of Education. Retrieved from nces.ed.gov/programs/coe/indicator_cgg.asp

National Center for Education Statistics. (2018c). Table 204.20. English language learner (ELL) students enrolled in public elementary and secondary schools, by state; selected years, fall 2000 through fall 2015. *Digest of education statistics.* U.S. Department of Education. Retrieved from nces.ed.gov/programs/digest/d17/tables/dt17_204.20.asp

National Center for Education Statistics. (2018d). Table 204.27. English language learner (ELL) students enrolled in public elementary and secondary schools, by grade, home language, and selected student characteristics: Selected years, 2008–09 through fall 2015. *Digest of education statistics.* U.S. Department of Education. Retrieved from nces.ed.gov/programs/digest/d17/tables/dt17_204.27.asp

National Center for Education Statistics. (2018e). English language learners in public schools. U.S. Department of Education. Retrieved from nces.ed.gov/programs/coe/indicator_cgf.asp

National Clearinghouse for English Language Acquisition. (2015). *Fast facts: Profiles of English Learners.* U.S. Department of Education. Retrieved from ncela.ed.gov/files/fast_facts/OELA_FastFacts_ProfilesOfELs.pdf

Noel, A., Stark, P., & Redford, J. (2016). *Parent and family involvement in education, from the National Household Education Surveys Program of 2012* (NCES 2013–028.REV2). National Center for Education Statistics, Institute of Education Sciences. U.S. Department of Education. Retrieved from nces.ed.gov/pubs2013/2013028rev.pdf

Office for Civil Rights, U.S. Department of Education. (2013–14a). 2013–14 Retention estimations by grade. Civil Rights Data Collection. Retrieved from http://ocrdata.ed.gov

Office for Civil Rights, U.S. Department of Education. (2013–14b). Number and percentage of public school students with disabilities served under IDEA overall and by race/ethnicity, and those who are English language learners, by state: School year 2013–14. Civil Rights Data Collection. Retrieved from http://ocrdata.ed.gov

Office for Civil Rights, U.S. Department of Education. (2013–14c). Public school students overall and by race/ethnicity, students with disabilities served under IDEA and those served solely under Section 504, and students who are English language learners, by state: School year 2013–14. Retrieved from http://ocrdata.ed.gov

Office of English Language Acquisition. (2015, January). *Fast facts: Profiles of English learners.* U.S. Department of Education. Retrieved from www2.ed.gov/about/offices/list/oela/fast-facts/pel.pdf

Office of English Language Acquisition. (2018, April). *Fast facts: Profiles of English learners.* U.S. Department of Education. Retrieved from ncela.ed.gov/files/fast_facts/Profiles_of_ELs_4.12.18_MM_Final_Edit.pdf

Owens, J. (2014). *Policy statement: School start times for adolescents.* American Academy of Pediatrics. Retrieved from pediatrics.aappublications.org/content/134/3/642

Perkins, I., & Flores, A. (2002). Mathematical notations and procedures of recent immigrant students. *Mathematics Teaching in the Middle School, 7*(6), 346–351. Retrieved from www.nctm.org/Publications/uncategorized/Mathematical-Notations-and-Procedures_pdf/

Potochnick, S. (2018). The academic adaptation of immigration students with interrupted schooling, *American Educational Research Journal, 55*(4), 859–892.

Recht, D., & Leslie L. (1988). Effect of prior knowledge on good and poor readers' memory of text, *Journal of Educational Psychology, 80,* 16–20.

Robinson, K., & Harris, A. L. (2014). *The broken compass: Parental involvement with children's education.* Cambridge, MA: Harvard University Press.

Rodrigues, J., & Pandeirada, J. (2018). When visual stimulation of the surrounding environment affects children's cognitive performance. *Journal of Experimental Child Psychology, 176,* 140–149.

Saunders, W., & Marcelletti, D. (2013). The gap that can't go away: The catch-22 of reclassification in monitoring the progress of English learners. *Educational Evaluation and Policy Analysis, 35*(2), 139–156.

Schwerdt, G., West, M., & Winters, M. (2017). *The effects of test-based retention on student outcomes over time: Regression discontinuity evidence from Florida.* National Bureau of Economic Research Working Paper No. 21509. Retrieved from www.nber.org/papers/w21509.pdf

Short, D., & Fitzsimmons, S. (2007). *Double the work: Challenges and solutions to acquiring language and academic literacy for adolescent English language learners.* Carnegie Corporation of New York. Retrieved from: www.carnegie.org/media/filer_public/bd/d8/bdd80ac7-fb48-4b97-b082-df8c49320acb/ccny_report_2007_double.pdf

Suskind, D. (2015). *Thirty million words: Building a child's brain.* New York: Dutton.

Thomas, W., & Collier, V. (1997). *School effectiveness for language minority students.* Washington, DC: National Clearinghouse for Bilingual Education. Retrieved from http://www.thomasandcollier.com/assets/1997_thomas-collier97-1.pdf

Thompson, K. (2015). English learners' time to reclassification: An analysis. *Educational Policy, 31,* 330–363.

Umansky, I. M., et al. (2016). *Improving the opportunities and outcomes of California's students learning English: Findings from school district–university collaborative partnerships,* Policy Brief 15.1. Policy Analysis for California Education, Stanford University. Retrieved from www.edpolicyinca.org/sites/default/files/PACE Policy Brief 15-1_v6.pdf

The Urban Institute. (2019). Data from the Integrated Public Use Microdata Series datasets drawn from the 2016 and 2017 American Community Survey. Retrieved from www.urban.org

U.S. Census Bureau. (2015). Census bureau reports at least 350 languages spoken in U.S. homes. Retrieved from www.census.gov/newsroom/press-releases/2015/cb15-185.html

U.S. Department of Education. (2016). *Non-regulatory guidance: English learners and Title III of the Elementary and Secondary Education Act (ESEA), as amended by the Every Student Succeeds Act (ESSA).* Retrieved from www2.ed.gov/policy/elsec/leg/essa/essatitleiiiguidenglishlearners92016.pdf

U.S. Department of Education. (2017). *English learner tool kit for state and local education agencies.* Retrieved from ncela.ed.gov/files/english_learner_toolkit/OELA_2017_ELsToolkit_508C.pdf

U.S. Department of Education. (2018). Teacher shortage areas. Retrieved from tsa.ed.gov

U.S. Department of Education, Office for Civil Rights, and U.S. Department of Justice, Civil Rights Division. (2015). *Dear colleague letter.* Retrieved from www2.ed.gov/about/offices/list/ocr/letters/colleague-el-201501.pdf

Weyer, M. (2018, June). A look at third grade reading retention policies. National Conference of State Legislatures. *LegisBrief, 26*(21). Retrieved from www.ncsl.org/documents/legisbriefs/2018/june/LBJune2018_A_Look_at_Third_Grade_Reading_Retention_Policies_goID32459.pdf

What Works Clearinghouse (2013, January). WWC review of the report "Same-language-subtitling (SLS): Using subtitled music video for reading growth." Institute of Education Sciences, U.S. Department of Education. Retrieved from ies.ed.gov/ncee/wwc/Docs/SingleStudyReviews/wwc_sls_010813.pdf

WIDA Consortium. (2007). *Access for ELLs: Interpreting the results*, Slide #23. Madison, WI: Wisconsin Center for Education Research. Retrieved from https://slideplayer.com/slide/7336208/https://slideplayer.com/slide/7336208/

WIDA Consortium. (2016). *K–12 can do descriptors, key uses edition grades 2–3*. Madison, WI: Wisconsin Center for Education Research. Retrieved from wida.wisc.edu/sites/default/files/resource/CanDo-KeyUses-Gr-2-3.pdf

WIDA Consortium. (2017a). *Consortium report*. Madison, WI: Wisconsin Center for Education Research. Retrieved from wida.wisc.edu/sites/default/files/Website/Memberships/Consortium/Annual-Reports/2017WIDAAnnualReport.pdf

WIDA Consortium. (2017b). *Identifying ELLs with specific learning disabilities*. Madison, WI: Wisconsin Center for Education Research. Retrieved from wida.wisc.edu/sites/default/files/resource/FocusOn-Identifying-ELLs-with-Specific-Learning-Disabilities.pdf

WIDA Consortium. (2018). *Spring 2018 interpretive guide for score reports kindergarten–grade 12*, p. 10. Madison, WI: Wisconsin Center for Education Research. Retrieved from wida.wisc.edu/sites/default/files/resource/Interpretive-Guide.pdf

Wilde, J. (2010). *Comparing results of the NAEP long-term trend assessment: ELLs, former ELLs, and English-proficient students*. Denver, CO: American Educational Research Association. Retrieved from citeseerx.ist.psu.edu/viewdoc/download;jsessionid=FC24D7E5846230FDB8963EC15BC5C5CA?doi=10.1.1.177.3912&rep=rep1&type=pdf

Willingham, D. (2006–2007, Winter). The usefulness of *brief* instruction in reading comprehension strategies. *American Educator*. Retrieved from https://www.aft.org/sites/default/files/periodicals/CogSci.pdf

Willingham, D., & Lovette, G. (2014, September 26). Can reading comprehension be taught? *Teachers College Record*. Retrieved from www.danielwillingham.com/uploads/5/0/0/7/5007325/willingham&lovette_2014_can_reading_comprehension_be_taught_.pdf

Wiswell, J. (2015, August). Super student: Refugee shines with success, *The Chaldean News*, pp. 25 and 39. Retrieved from issuu.com/chaldeannews/docs/cn0815_0148_locked

Zong, J., & Batalova, J. (2015). *The limited English proficient population in the United States*. Migration Policy Institute. Retrieved from www.migrationpolicy.org/article/limited-english-proficient-population-united-states

Index

The letter *f* following a page number denotes a figure.

About the Author

Barbara Gottschalk, as a full-time, in-the-trenches educator, taught English language learners from first graders to graduate students in five states in three very different parts of the United States. After teaching English in Japan early in her career, she earned an M.A. in teaching English to speakers of other languages (TESOL) as well as an MBA. She was an invited speaker on ELL issues for the 30th Annual High Schools That Work Development Conference and has presented numerous times at the International TESOL conference and at conferences for state affiliates MITESOL, Ohio TESOL, and Kansas TESOL. A two-year stint representing English language learner interests as one of 160 fellows in America Achieves, a national educator organization, elevated her voice further. She wrote and implemented many successful grants for her school and has served as a grant reviewer for TESOL, her professional organization, as well as for the U.S. Department of Education's Office of English Language Acquisition. Her first book, *Get Money for Your Classroom: Easy Grant Writing Ideas that Work,* was published by Routledge in 2017.

Related ASCD Resources: English Language Learners

At the time of publication, the following resources were available (ASCD stock numbers appear in parentheses):

Print Products

Success with Multicultural Newcomers & English Learners: Proven Practices for School Leadership Teams by Margarita Espino Calderón and Shawn Slakk (#117026)

Classroom Instruction That Works with English Language Learners, 2nd Edition by Jane D. Hill and Kirsten B. Miller (#114004)

Assessing Multilingual Learners: A Month-by-Month Guide (ASCD Arias) by Margo Gottlieb (#SF117076)

Classroom Instruction That Works with English Language Learners Facilitator's Guide by Jane D. Hill and Cynthia L. Björk (#108052)

Classroom Instruction That Works with English Language Learners Participant's Workbook by Jane D. Hill and Cynthia L. Björk (#108053)

Getting Started with English Language Leaners: How Educators Can Meet the Challenge by Judie Haynes (#106048)

The Language-Rich Classroom: A Research-Based Framework for Teaching English Language Learners by Persida Himmele and William Himmele (#108037)

Reaching Out to Latino Families of English Language Learners by David Campos, Rocio Delgago, and Mary Esther Soto Huerta (#110005)

Strategies for Success with English Language Learners: An ASCD Action Tool by Virginia Pauline Rohas (#111061)

Productive Group Work: How to Engage Students, Build Teamwork, and Promote Understanding by Nancy Frey, Douglas Fisher, and Sandi Everlove (#109018)

Teaching English Language Learners Across the Content Areas by Judie Haynes and Debbie Zacarian (#109032)

For up-to-date information about ASCD resources, go to www.ascd.org. You can search the complete archives of *Educational Leadership* at www.ascd.org/el.

ASCD myTeachSource®

Download resources from a professional learning platform with hundreds of research-based best practices and tools for your classroom at http://myteach-source.ascd.org/.

For more information, send an e-mail to member@ascd.org; call 1-800-933-2723 or 703-578-9600; send a fax to 703-575-5400; or write to Information Services, ASCD, 1703 N. Beauregard St., Alexandria, VA 22311-1714 USA.

THE WHOLE CHILD

The ASCD Whole Child approach is an effort to transition from a focus on narrowly defined academic achievement to one that promotes the long-term development and success of all children. Through this approach, ASCD supports educators, families, community members, and policymakers as they move from a vision about educating the whole child to sustainable, collaborative actions.

Dispelling Misconceptions About English Language Learners relates to the **engaged, supported,** and **challenged** tenets. *For more about the ASCD Whole Child approach, visit* **www.ascd.org/wholechild.**

WHOLE CHILD
TENETS

1 HEALTHY
Each student enters school healthy and learns about and practices a healthy lifestyle.

2 SAFE
Each student learns in an environment that is physically and emotionally safe for students and adults.

3 ENGAGED
Each student is actively engaged in learning and is connected to the school and broader community.

4 SUPPORTED
Each student has access to personalized learning and is supported by qualified, caring adults.

5 CHALLENGED
Each student is challenged academically and prepared for success in college or further study and for employment and participation in a global environment.

LEARN. TEACH. LEAD.